Personality, Spirit,
and Ethics

American University Studies

Series V
Philosophy

Vol. 181

PETER LANG
New York • Washington, D.C./Baltimore • Boston
Bern • Frankfurt am Main • Berlin • Vienna • Paris

Howard A. Slaatté

Personality, Spirit, and Ethics

The Ethics of Nicholas Berdyaev

PETER LANG
New York • Washington, D.C./Baltimore • Boston
Bern • Frankfurt am Main • Berlin • Vienna • Paris

Library of Congress Cataloging-in-Publication Data

Slaatté, Howard Alexander.
Personality, spirit, and ethics: the ethics of Nicholas Berdyaev/
Howard A. Slaatté.
p. cm. — (American university studies. Series V, Philosophy; v. 181)
Includes bibliographical references and index.
1. Berdiaev, Nikolai, 1874–1948—Ethics. I. Title. II. Series: American
university studies. Series V, Philosophy; vol. 181.
B4238.B44S54   170'.92—dc20   96-42959
ISBN 0-8204-3671-2
ISSN 0739-6392

Die Deutsche Bibliothek-CIP-Einheitsaufnahme

Slaatté, Howard A.:
Personality, spirit, and ethics: the ethics of Nicholas Berdyaev/
Howard A. Slaatté. –New York; Washington, D.C./Baltimore; Bern; Frankfurt
am Main; Berlin; Vienna; Paris: Lang.
(American university studies; Ser. 5, Philosophy; Vol. 181)
ISBN 0-8204-3671-2
NE: American university studies/ 05

The paper in this book meets the guidelines for permanence and durability
of the Committee on Production Guidelines for Book Longevity
of the Council of Library Resources.

© 1997 Peter Lang Publishing, Inc., New York

Printed in the United States of America.

Table of Contents

Preface

It can be said with candor that Nicholas Berdyaev became one of the shrewdest and most philosophically creative ethicists of this century. Despite his Bolshevik background he became a pro-Christian philosopher, who not only criticized Russia's Communist regime but led many students to re-appraise what philosophy in general was about and Christian philosophy in particular.

When Berdyaev came to see the weaknesses of materialistic brands of thought centering around a lack of ethical consider-ations and the existential meaning of life, he did not hesitate to espouse respect for a view of life embracing spiritual reali-ties. Despite his militaristic background he turned away from its glamour to a more independent perspective of life and so-ciety combined with respect for existential and Christian per-spectives.

At first Berdyaev, as a student influenced by a Kantian in-terpretation of ethics, became sympathetic with the Bolshevik revolution of 1917 to overthrow the Czar. In time he was made Professor of Philosophy at the University of Moscow (Kiev). During the 1920's he became outspoken against the unethical tactics of the Communists of the young Soviet Union. He was imprisoned and twice exiled to Siberia. Upon his return he was still critical of the Marxist regime, and in 1927 he fled to Claremont, a suburb of Paris, and lived there, first with his wife and later in the home of his sister-in-law, Madame Rapp.

During the period Berdyaev wrote numerous works making impacts upon the intelligentsia of Europe and America. In 1948 Cambridge University awarded him an honorary degree shortly before his death. The "White Russians," who sought more democratic opportunities in the West, looked to Berdyaev for both intellectual and spiritual leadership as one who understood their heritage and the cultures of both sides of the Iron Curtain. Berdyaev became a renowned thinker respected not only by philosophers but theologians as well.

Despite minimal religious background in his youth, Berdyaev moved more and more toward Christian thought and influenced many to think and re-think what an ethical and spiritual philosophy entailed. Though he became sympathetic with various socialist views of culture, as a philosopher he observed that the Marxists lacked genuine respect for human personality, its creativeness and moral freedom of spirit. Also, Berdyaev rejected the materialistic views of man among prevalent psychologies. Man to him was primarily a conscious, free and creative being, hence, all reductionistic views of man, he felt, must be relinquished.

Ethical values became for Berdyaev his main concerns and intellectual priorities. Man, being more than a creature of nature, was to be viewed as created *imago dei*. Not absorbed by the immanence of nature and of God, man encountered faithwise the divine as transcendent. Man encountered God in a faith-conditioned relationship, which became highly relevant to Berdyaev, existentially. A meaningful life is realized in the present moment of faith when the person is encountered by God even as eternity meets him in his time. This encounter is akin to the New Testament *Kairos*, which regenerates ordinary *chronos* and redeems *Historie*, thus making for a *Heilsgeschichte* of Spirit-inspired life and culture. A meaningful life is always in the present as it looks to eternal love, freedom and creativity.

When I studied at Mansfield College, Oxford, my first piece of research was on Berdyaev's epistemology, which I submitted to Dr. Evgueny Lampert, a friend and student of Berdyaev, who submitted my work to Oxford University leaders who filed the manuscript with their masters' theses. I became acquainted with people around Oxford who had been friends of Berdyaev, and I met with some of them in their homes. Later I met his closest friend, Peter Pianoff, in Paris, who conducted me to the little Orthodox church where Berdyaev worshipped. I found it a privilege to visit with Berdyaev's sister-in-law, Madame Rapp, even as I sat at his desk, which was just as he had left it.

Howard A. Slaatté, Ph.D.

Professor Emeritus
Marshall University
Huntington, West Virginia, U.S.A.

Courtesy Professor
University of South Florida
Tampa, Florida, U.S.A.

The Oak Knoll
Spring Hill, FL 34609

PART ONE

PERSONALITY AND EXISTENTIAL ISSUES

Chapter I

Personality and Its Meaning

Personality is the *expressed self*. It is the person's degree of development in relation to his moral nature as spirit and to all phases of experience, especially with other selves.

By virtue of its intrinsic nature personality can be described adequately only in terms of the self, the spirit of life, which with all its subtle individuality makes you "you." This makes it the individual person in process of self-realization from within everyday existence.

Contrary to the ancient Greek "persona" or mask used in drama, the personality is not only one's *self* as others see you but as you see yourself and as you really are under God. Personality is the ever changing, yet permanent, self in process of becoming more mature. Since the self is a spirit-subject which is the most basic form of life, while more than organic yet related thereto, it is essential to think of it in process of growth. Changing, it is either developing or degenerating, fulfilling its potentialities or betraying itself. Not permanent, personality is the self which undergoes change. Only a spiritual concept of selfhood can do justice to this paradox. This combination of permanence and unity with change and multiplicity implies the distinctiveness of every person. There is an individuality about it which implies distinctive rational, emotional, intuitive and dispositional bents, tastes or preferences. These are developed, uncovered or intensified by experience and pertain to all of life's undertakings or anticipations as they relate themselves to everything from physical impulse and material pursuits to things ethical, aesthetic and spiritual.

Personality demands that the self be related to other selves.
The more the normal self is exposed to other selves the more
its personality is allowed to develop from the seed and bud of
potentiality to the blossom of maturity. For the spirit-self to
realize itself there must be the social fellowship with other
selves to bring forth the needed self-expression implicit in
personality development. At best self-expression is a form of
communication regardless of what form it takes; thus, other
selves are essential to the self and its expression. In so far as
self-expression gradually becomes more complex it develops
more consideration for others in the light of the commonly
accepted social mores, moral principles and permanent standards of their social culture. This is the moral side of personality development which may be described as character. From
this perspective personality can never be limited to a mere
winsomeness of manner, a finesse of poise or a style of dress
or procedure.

Just as the person or self is in essence a spiritual and conscious knowing subject, philosophically speaking, so, too, personality is in essence a spiritual phenomenon. The principles with which it must reckon in relation to other selves are
in the last analysis either intuited or accepted on faith. In view
of this, personality is the self-expression and development of
not a mere organism but of a being of moral and spiritual
dimensions. As such, a person subsumes his body and mind
under the spirit or orients them around the Spirit-Self of God,
the cosmic Pneuma.

Nicholas Berdyaev saw personality to be more than biological individuality linked with self-preservation. It is rather "the
image of God," not as of an abstract monotheism or idealism
but as the Spirit-Being of love understood as sacrifice. This is
not an abstract essence but a personhood. Personality by its
nature presupposes a "Thou" or another self.[1] It is self-giving
to others, hence, at its best it is Agape as in I John. Personality
is of the highest value; it is anchored in "the moral principle"
basic to ethics, since all other values are based upon it.[2]

Berdyaev sees a variety of ethics including "creative ethics"
which is based on the principle of self-giving love and sacrifice (Agape). It's the answer to humanism, which sees self-per-
fectibility as the supreme value. Christianity provides a refer-
ence point from beyond the self toward others.

Berdyaev could see that a personality had to have a spiritual element making him/her independent of the determinisms of both nature and society. This spiritual element usually called spirit embraces the completeness of personality with both bodily functions and the soul. Hence it introduces one to a higher order of existence. Though the body belongs to personality, the spiritual element of a person cannot be abstracted from the body. Even the form of the body signifies a victory of spirit over formless matter. Expanded, this also implies mind over matter, even cosmic in form.

Personality is a spiritual phenomenon. It is not subordinate to society but quite the reverse, existentially. Society is an expressed aspect of personality, so the world is a social aspect of personality. The existential center is not society or nature but personality, for it is the knowing subject, not the object, which is the center of existence. As Berdyaev states, "Personality has its roots in the spiritual world; its existence presupposes an (ethical) dualism of spirit and nature, of freedom and determinism, of the individual and the general, of the kingdom of God and the kingdom of Caesar. The existence of human personality in the world shows that the world is not self-sufficient, that it must be transcended and find completion not in itself but in God, in super-cosmic being."[3] This implies a higher type of existence than found in nature, though not totally disparate from it. It implies that personality is more than the biological individual; it is a freedom of spirit related to God as Spirit.

Personality is a combination of unity and multiplicity as well as permanence and change. More than a coordination thereof, it is a unified whole. Paradoxically personality is the unchanging subject of changes i.e. an unchanging core which develops through changes. "Personality," says Berdyaev, "is, above all, the unity of destiny; and destiny means change, development, and preservation of the existential center. This is the mystery of personality."[4] It is of a super-personal existence reflecting intrinsic super-personal values.

Not self-sufficient, personality must relate itself to other personalities and to the cosmos and God. Not merely a particular phenomenon, "personality must be filled with universal content." As an act it is a process of "creating itself." "It is God's idea of what a man ought to be." It is an "unending process of creativeness."[5] The active element in man is spirit, not merely life, which is quite passive. Action makes for something new. As Berdyaev puts it, non-existence becomes existence. Creativeness, then, implies freedom, not determinism. Personality is self-determination and resists nature's determinisms. Unlike the physical individual, personality is not only the consequence of natural and social processes but is created by God and is the source of dignity and freedom. Personality is the opposite of sheer conformity such as imposed on us by the pressures of nature and society. It is the paradoxical combination of opposites like the finite and infinite, freedom and destiny, the super-personal and the personal, the permanent and the changing. Paradoxically, in order to be creative personality must already exist. Yet it must be social if it is to have a realized dignity and fulfillment.

Notes

1. Cf. Martin Buber, *I and Thou*, a work supporting much of Berdyaev's existential personalism.

2. *Ibid.*

3. Nicolas Berdyaev, "Marxism And The Conception of Personality" *Christendom*, Oxford (Blackwell) Vol. V, no. 20. December, 1935 and Vol. VI, no. 21, March 1976, pp. 251–262, pp. 35–40, respectively.

4. *Ibid*, p. 253f.

5. *Ibid.*

Chapter II

Personality and Consciousness

Berdyaev views man as the key to the mystery of both existence and knowledge. Though a part of nature, man is not fully
explainable thereby. Even so man is the major clue to being.
Man is the bearer of meaning, even though he is a fallen creature in whom meaning is distorted. But since a fall implies
from a height, man's fall is "a token of his greatness," says
Berdyaev. Similarly Blaise Pascal would say that man's awareness of his fall is a sign of his greatness. Berdyaev also implies
that man's fallen state retains the mark of greatness, for he is
capable of a higher life and knowledge, which rises above the
lesser to meaningless things of the world.

Essential to knowledge is the knowledge of God himself in
his Spirit. But objectified reasoning cannot bring this about
since not in touch with Spirit.[1] Spirit is not an object. In philosophy there is an inner kinship between the knower and the
known, which objectification does not provide. Basic is consciousness, which presupposes the subject-object relation even
as it transcends objectification. Consciousness seeks to rise to
a "super-consciousness" which evaluates things through "creative spiritual acts." Ethical insights are known only in this
way by the person involved. This perspective is a phenomenological one. Implied herein is the mystery of knowledge as
based on the conscious knower, who transcends the known.

Moral knowledge is not only viewed mentally but created
mentally. It is of the conscious knowing subject. It cannot be
objectified. To evaluate an object requires an evaluation, which
is a creative spiritual act fundamental to ethical judgment. "The

task of ethics is not to draw up a list of traditional norms but to have the daring to make creative evaluations," says Berdyaev.[2] Legalistic codes do not provide these. There is little value in abstract a priori ethics such as Platonic ideals or Kant's Categorical Imperative, lest ethics be reduced to intellectual concepts. More basic than such intellectual games is moral experience, though empirical ethics does not have the last word either. Ethics is not merely an academic exercise, it springs from concrete existence through creative evaluations. This makes it more prophetic than authoritative. Values must be re-evaluated regularly with "a critique of pure conscience, " as Berdyaev puts it.[3] This provides an axiological point-of-view of ethics. Yet this also makes for an ontological view, since values are considered a force in society and not merely abstract norms. Purposes and values derived from timeless ideals are unintelligible when imposed upon this world. Ethics is concerned with spiritual freedom and not natural necessity.[4] This freedom is very much interrelated with the social world.

Good and evil are to a great extent symbolic. Often "mythus" and biblical "types" are strong expressions thereof. Today ethical studies are dominated by sociological phenomena due to "the tyranny which social life and social norms exercise over the moral life of man." This is linked with the impersonalized view of society as held by Heidegger, which he calls *das Man* or "One." It is much like "the herd" to which individuals are pressed into by conformity. It is important that we take note that even if the distinction between good and evil were social in origin it would not determine "the nature of moral valuation." Ethical principles precede social experiences in principle and are brought to them. Ideas of good and evil may depend upon society but not good and evil themselves. As a spiritual being man can know the good; as a social being he knows only the changing conceptions of the good.[5] Valuation presupposes something beyond what is valued; hence, the spiritual interpretation presupposes the divine and is more basic than the social views. Ethics in this light becomes "the theory of the destiny and vocation of man," which includes inquiry into man's origin and goal, according to Berdyaev.[6]

In addition Berdyaev sees where ethics presupposes a theodicy, considering God as well as man. The problem of evil is recognized by theology but not solved thereby. To say that it is due to man's God-given freedom is superficial; it implies that freedom dooms man into perdition. This gives excuses for atheism. Berdyaev says that God did not make freedom; it is meonically of "the nothing" out of which God created the world, i.e. meonic freedom only as inert possibility. God, then, is not responsible for a freedom which occasioned evil, nor because he gave man freedom.

The so-called "second act" of God was one of redemption. God descended sacrificially into non-being, the abyss of freedom which has degenerated into evil. Divine sacrifice conquers both moral freedom and meonic freedom. The responsibility of evil does not degrade man but exalts him, for it implies that he comes from a pure state and has a freedom capable of rising against God and even separating himself from God. If man fell away from God he must have been endowed with a great capacity, that of freedom, and this exalted him, says Berdyaev. The fall was not by creation but by man's power even as a rebel. This bespeaks an element of dignity related to man's possession of freedom despite its abuse.[7]

Pantheism is wrong upon denying freedom, likewise a dualistic theism which only admits freedom to keep man morally responsible. Both monism and dualism compete with or deny freedom, for they are both deterministic. The antinomies of the Creator and the creature imply a paradox which neither category can handle. Another form of determinism is predestination, for it assumes Grace acts upon man independent of his freedom. Berdyaev declares that the only way out of these determinisms is to concede that freedom is "uncreated" as in his theory of meonic freedom with roots in non-being. Grace does not diminish freedom but elevates it. Human freedom alone cannot turn man to God, yet the influence of Grace does not coerce him; it is not determinative so much as persuasive. The underlying paradox of Grace and freedom is focused upon the mystery of Christ the God-man.[8] The good that penetrates the story of the Fall of man is that if man had remained perfectly in the paradise of Eden or the divinely natural life he would not have come to the knowledge of Christ. Here is another paradox, one which allows for a higher stage of human existence.

Ethics must consider the place for a philosophical anthropology. The natural and social sciences have not solved the problem and/or the meaning of man. Berdyaev maintains that a science of anthropology sheds less light than a philosophical anthropology, and he may be right, for a philosophical anthropology is holistic and is essential to ethics. Man must be understood first and last if the world is to be understood. All spheres of being intersect in man. So philosophy must be anthropological. Here Berdyaev is quite existential and personalistic.[9]

Man belongs to two worlds, the natural and the trans-natural or spiritual. It is the reason for man's antinomous nature and paradoxical existence. Not only fallen, man is reminiscent of the heaven from which he fell, which is to say he is also a child of God and a creative being helping to bring about a higher stage of life. Man can understand himself only in relation to God; hence religious consciousness alone can do justice to this. Philosophical anthropology calls for the aid of religious anthropology, its preliminary view. The gist of Christian anthropology is expressed by Berdyaev like this: Man is created by God in his image, intelligent and free, but has fallen away from fellowship with God, yet in his fallen and sinful condition man has received soteriological overtures from the Grace of God which is what redeems, regenerates, re-motivates and, in short, saves him. Christian anthropology sees the new Adam supplanting the old; it speaks of "new creatures in Christ," as St. Paul expressed it, and "old things have passed away and behold all things are made new." (II Cor. 5:17) The human quandary is overcome; the tragic and sinful man is granted hope and a new status.[10]

Berdyaev saw where thinkers like Shakespeare, Dostoevsky, Tolstoy, Augustine, Jacob Boehme, Pascal and Kierkegaard have done more for understanding human nature than the academic psychologists and sociologists of recent generations. Social thinkers like Comte, Marx and Durkheim catered to the moral consciousness of primitive man as if it were the height of manhood. Stressing the individual in the group they failed to accentuate personality as such. Their objective "socialization of man" depreciated human subjectivity, freedom of the spirit and conscience. Often "the enemy of personality is the com-

munity but not communality as Sobernost." Moral life is social "togetherness," but the basis thereof is spiritual; morals
are far more than mores or customs. Philosophically, it becomes wrong to say that the knowledge of good and evil is
either good or evil per se. Even a thinker like Marx refers to
good and evil, but he does not explain or even ask what they
mean apart from social practices and opinions. The source
and nature of values are overlooked.[11]

Surrounding these ethical claims is the view of C. S. Lewis
in *The Great Divorce* that the spiritually lost are not to be pit-
ied, for they have chosen their fate. This is comparable to
Berdyaev's view of destiny in relation to the alternatives of
heaven and hell or perdition and its opposite in eternal life or
heaven. Man's commitments affect his destiny. Yet a more
Christian view would allow for the pity for the lost, because
the lost are such largely out of decisions related to spiritual
ignorance and/or defeat. Should not Christian compassion
make possible a spiritual pity for those outside the spirit? Without it all forms of evangelism are apt to be weakened if not
negated.

It was Christianity which made the individual's moral life
basically independent of the tribe, clan or other social groups.
This writer often wonders where he would be had not the love
ethics of Christians converted the often harsh Vikings from
whom he descended. But the bold vengeance of primitive societies has been transferred to the state; capital punishment is
a survival thereof.[12]

The only anthropology that is eternal in quality is the Jew-
ish-Christian view of man as created by God in his image, but
it is not a complete picture of man, for he is divided by his
fallen, sinful condition. Yet it views man as a free and creative
spirit who transcends nature and is called to work for the build-
ing up of the world.[13]

Man is also an androgynous being, who must respect the
bifocal tensions between the male and female elements of existence. Only the union of the two makes for the wholeness of
human being. Berdyaev provocatively states, "Man sinks low,
overcome by the unregenerate force of sex, and rises high
through sublimating it. The concentrated power of sex may be
a source of creativeness. To sacrifice one's Eros, diverting its

energy in another direction, may increase one's creative power. We see it in Ibsen and the tragic fate of Kierkegaard, who sacrificed his love and found compensation in his creative genius." Kierkegaard psychologically regarded fear to be an essential characteristic of man's spirituality and relation to divine transcendence intensified by the fall. Psychopathology has helped clarify this, because it has seen man as a sick being with tensions between his consciousness and sub-consciousness. Consequentially, this is not unlike the idea of original sin; man is divided or split. Berdyaev says that human nature is rooted in fathomless, pre-existential meonic freedom, which is often presupposed by God and belief in God. But the mature Christian view of man is a holistic view based on two theories; (a) man is the likeness of God, and (b) God became man in the God-man.[14]

Consciousness and the subconscious mind are commonly in a state of tension; hence, the psychologist Alfred Adler says man always seeks to compensate himself. A person may support a law, for instance, which has not been supported by his sub-conscious mind. Also, though man is egoistical, it does not mean that he loves only himself. The most vindictive people are those who do not love themselves. Those who have some liking for themselves are usually kinder toward others. The persons who are proud and touchey do not love themselves; those who do have legitimate self love usually have self-respect.[15] Did not Jesus see how this is related to an expendable and outgoing love? One cannot love others if he hates himself.

Imagination is an important epistemological human capacity. It makes for creativity in both the arts and sciences. It is more than imitation of ideal forms or patterns, for it is creation from the depths of non-being even bringing forth images which have not previously existed. It is a product of the unconscious, yet the unconscious plays a double role; not only the source of creativeness it is also the source of neurosis, says Berdyaev. Psycho-pathology sees many nervous diseases linked with moral conflicts to be caused by "the thwarting of the unconscious and its primeval instincts."[16]

Rationalism is unaware of the mystery of sublimation which implies that both naive idealism and naive materialism do not reckon with the mystery of the subconscious, while "spiritual victories are won in the domain of superconsciousness, i.e. in the spirit, and not in consciousness." Accordingly, moral recoveries are made, says Berdyaev. Relative to this "the Christian doctrine of grace has always meant recovery of spiritual health, which law cannot bring about, but it has not been utilized as a basis for ethics."[17] An exception would be the book *A New Heaven And A New Earth* by Edwin Lewis.

Berdyaev also sees how creativity is a means of healing. He distinguishes three forms of ethics. (1) the ethics of law, (2) the ethics of redemption, (3) the ethics of creativeness. Each type helps awaken the human spirit by creative spiritual power rather than by laws and norms. The ethics of law commonly represses the subconsciousness and knows nothing of the liberating superconsciousness. It is based upon fear, which Christians see to be the result of original sin; it implies danger, which vitiates human existence. The spiritual superconsciousness places man above nature while depriving it of demonic powers as it "de-mentalizes nature," says Berdyaev. Consciousness is the arena of man's struggles between his spirit and nature. The meaning and relevance of redemption is the strongest healing factor, for it awakens the spirit and leads to creativeness, the completion of redemption. Here we have the basic conception of the dynamic type of ethics perpetrated by Nicholas Berdyaev.[18]

Free will, Berdyaev believes, is not an element of the mental life which chooses between good and evil and makes man responsible for evil. Such a view springs from "utilitarian pedagogical considerations," he says, while within it free will is not creative and keeps a person in a perpetual state of anxiety, tension or fear. True liberation is wrought through grace and not free will.[19] But the Arminian view of grace sees it capable of allowing free will to respond to its loving overtures. Berdyaev comes close to this and thereby sees Grace making for a spiritual fellowship. The purpose of life is not as inspiring of dignity as is the source from which one's moral life and activity spring. The motive and spirit in which one acts is more important than the ends pursued. The moral good is not a goal but an inner energy and attitude which speaks throughout one's existence. By this God expresses himself in the world through interaction with man as man answers God's call.[20]

Berdyaev recognizes opposites at work in man but not as due to the Fall but to the duality of human nature from the outset. He states, "The creature cannot fall away from the Creator, it cannot have the strength to do so, it cannot even think of it." Rather, the Fall is due to possibilities included in the uncreated or pre-created freedom which Berdyaev refers to as meonic. This implies that original sin was not a willful rebellion on the part of man's will against God; it was an existential condition with undetermined possibilities.[21]

Yet individuality is a naturalistic category while personality is that and more, for it is a spiritual one. Berdyaev, therefore, sees the need of a personalistic ethics from the perspective of concrete existence, hence it must be of existential perspective. Personality is not generated by man but created by God with room for individual development and achievement. Under God it is a wholeness and is of eternal worth, axiologically. It is the *imago dei* and is the highest value in the world. While itself a value it bears so-called "super-personal values" under divine inspiration.

"If there is no God, as the source of superpersonal values," Berdyaev says, "personality as a value does not exist either; there is merely the individual entity subordinate to the natural life of the genus." Morals, after all, are based on personality, and there cannot be an impersonal ethics. Freedom, value and tragedy have significance only for persons. "The life of personality is not self-preservation as that of the individual but self-development and self-determination. The very existence of personality presupposes sacrifice, and sacrifice cannot be impersonal." Contrary to Scheler, personality is not self-contained. It presupposes other selves, lest it become disintegrated. Even the Holy Trinity, spiritually speaking, is a trinity of persons which presuppose one another and imply mutual love and communion, says Berdyaev. As personalities God and man presuppose each other. Even God "needs his other, for God is Agape, and He shares that expendable love. God is not conceivable as merely an abstract monotheism. Personalistic ethics is based upon the metaphysics of the Trinity. Personality is basic yet not linked with original sin, lest it be a "hardened selfhood." Berdyaev states that it is only when such selfhood melts spiritually under transcendence that personality is manifested.[22]

Neither individualistic nor universal ethics can solve the underlying problems of the individual and society. Psychoanalysis is inadequate, for ultimate truths elude it. It overly stresses sexual life and fails to include the remission of sins and spiritual regeneration. It moralizes without knowing what sin is and its source. Freud exaggerates man's ignorance of his unconscious drives. Freud's chief merit, however, is his discovery of the evil part played by consciousness. Akin to this Dostoevsky has shown that man is an irrational being who is inclined, for example, to be both masochistic and sadistic.[23]

Berdyaev sees that ethics must be based on "creative freedom as the source of life." The basic issue is not freedom and necessity but freedom and grace. Ethics is not based on the separation of God and man. It must neither be humanistic nor theological but "theo-andric" as it looks to the God-man or the divinely human principle focused in Christ; in this respect it is bi-polar, as Berdyaev emphasizes. He also underlines St. Paul's claim that man cannot attain righteousness by law, though the law clarifies what sin is. "Man is justified by faith without the deeds of the law," says Paul, (Galatians 2:16; Romans 3:24). Yet this does not mean that St. Paul promoted antinomianism. He saw Grace to be beyond law. Yet the ethics of law co-exists with that of redemption and creativeness. Often Christian ethics has slipped into legalism either ecclesiastical or pietistic. The ethics of law tends to be socially applied rather than personally related to redemptive ethics and creativeness. The herd morality is catered to under law, it is social in character like the *das Man* of Heidegger while impersonal in form.[24] This means that social domination through laws and norms overwhelms the inwardly personal uniqueness of the individual and his conscience.

The ethics of law must be transcended to vindicate the creativity of personality. It is a paradox because it also has a positive value of its own.[25] Socrates did not rise above the ethics of law any more than the Stoics, says Berdyaev, but he advanced the moral liberation of personality and personal conscience as distinct from social mores and pressures. "When Plato in the *Gorgias* says that it is better to suffer injustice than to inflict it on others, he transfers the center of gravity in moral life to the depths of personality."[26] The weakness of legal ethics is its appeal to fear. It does not re-motivate persons from within or regenerate human nature or destroy sin but only keeps it within bounds. Even laws in idealistic settings, which assert the value of personality, tend to be abstract. Kant had an abstract and normative conception of personality when he held to a system which minimized individuality. Berdyaev touches a tender nerve in this context when he says, "The terrible thing about moralism is that it strives to make man into an automaton of virtue."[27] Kant is at fault here in seeking a normative ethics which is autonomous. Yet he must be credited with keeping ethical philosophy alive and helping to re-condition modern thought around moral virtues. This has done much, indirectly, to awaken the secular world to greater respect for the religious dimension of life and the need to retain strong moral and social responsibilities within the religious community as well. But the ethical sensitivities of religion are much more realizeable when men yield to divine Grace and are inwardly re-oriented and re-motivated by the higher levels of morality linked with Christ and his ethics of sacrificial love.

Notes

1. Berdyaev, *Destiny of Man*, pp. 11-13.

2. *Ibid*, pp. 14, 16.

3. *Ibid*, pp. 15, 16, 17.

4. *Ibid*, pp. 16-18.

5. *Ibid*, pp. 18-20.

6. *Ibid*, pp. 20-22.

7. *Ibid*, pp. 24-26. For "meonic freedom" see Chapter 8 below.

8. *Ibid*, pp. 27-36.

9. *Ibid*, pp. 36-40; 40ff.

10. *Ibid*, pp. 40-45f.

11. *Ibid*, pp. 47-49; 55-58.

12. *Ibid*, p. 49f.

13. *Ibid*, p. 60f, 49.

14. *Ibid*, pp.49f.

15. *Ibid*, pp. 49, 60f, 62, 65.

16. *Ibid*, pp. 71, 75.

17. *Ibid*, p. 78.

18. *Ibid*, pp. 77ff.

19. *Ibid*, 79f.

20. *Ibid*, p. 54f.

21. *Ibid*, pp. 54f.

22. *Ibid*, p. 57-58.

23. *Ibid*, p. 23f.

24. *Ibid*, pp. 75–82.

25. *Ibid*, pp. 93–94.

26. *Ibid*, pp. 93f.

27. *Ibid*, p. 95.

Chapter III

Personality and Spirit

The idea of personality springs from Christian faith, love and experience. Christianity, says Bishop F. R. Barry of Southwell, is "the religion of personality more than any other religion." Quite like Berdyaev, he says the persons of the triune godhead imply that personality in God and man can enter into relationships. Many people accept Jesus' Sermon on the Mount but overlook the fact that it presupposes a loving God called Father to whom we must respond freely. Many believe that what is impersonal is to be reverenced more than what is personal, hence, to them, the word 'it' is regarded as better than 'He.' But the Church cannot accept this, lest Christian ethics be repudiated along with its social mission. Personality is basic to both. Human dignity and human rights spring from this.

Basic to biblical faith personality "reflects the highest level of revelation in the self-disclosure of God to man," as Berdyaev puts it, for it reflects "the loving God" and is "the most important contribution of Christianity to metaphysics."[1] Not merely a rational first Cause or divine Absolute this implies a living or active God, as the prophetic movement presupposes God as self-disclosed through persons. The New Testament emphasis, "God is love," also implies personality. The living God is personal subject, not mere concept or object.[2] Berdyaev would support Barry's claims here.

Berdyaev's book *Freedom And The Spirit* is one which exposes his inner self as a thinker who has travelled far in the realms of spirit and reflects his shifts in the search for truth. For him new spiritual territories are taken in the search for reality. One of his major victories was over humanism, another was over authoritarianism. It was liberty of the spirit that brought him to God and his freedom.

Religion, Berdyaev maintained, cannot rest on abstractions or compulsions. Vital spiritual experience authenticates this; it is freely expressed. Speaking existentially, Berdyaev states, "I admit that it is grace which has brought me to faith, but it is grace experienced by me as freedom."[3] This is to be understood in view of the Spirit and three stages of religious life, as Berdyaev speaks of it. (a) Popular objective systems of religion. (b) Subjective individualistic or pietistic experience. (c) The opposition between them as transcended in the highest type of spirituality. The latter provides society with a spiritual aristocracy though not as a classistic notion or anti-democratic view of the Church, Gnostic or otherwise. Besides spiritual liberation of the individual there is the spirit and practice of *Sobornost*, the Russian term for "togetherness" or fraternal catholicity and brotherhood, which is basic to the *Koivwvia* of the church.[4]

Spiritual persons should never boast of their spirituality as a superiority over natural men. Actually they are often less happy because of the extra personal and social burdens they choose to assume and the inner tensions related thereto. Often they are lonely persons, too. The Gnostics failed to see Christian salvation as offered to everyone. They failed to grasp the mystery of freedom as freedom in Christ with love.

Berdyaev would not embrace the gnostic dualism. He saw evil to be spiritual, not merely carnal, but as a lesser quality of spirit. Hence, he thinks prophetically moreso than scientifically, i.e. as a Christian theosophist who creatively poses problems more than providing pre-established answers. This approach sharpens Christian consciousness rather than providing an abstract metaphysics. It makes Berdyaev more like Pascal than philosophers who abstractly hypostatize psychic and material phenomena, then systematize them as ontological substances. For such thinkers even God is assumed to be a metaphysical substance of a rational nature. Hegel is the worst proponent of such rational projections. For him God and reason are of the same cosmic order of reality,[5] viz *nous* rather than *pneuma*.

Though German idealism counteracted naturalistic meta-physics, Berdyaev could see that it made progress toward "the knowledge of the spirit," because it was more dynamic than naturalism and made way for spiritual life, despite its abstract features. Thomism's naive realism is deemed erroneous, too, because it makes God just another object of nature. Berdyaev rejected this Aristotelian view of God as *actus purus*, for it deprives God of an inner life, as it reduces God to a lifeless object. This naturalistic metaphysics makes it impossible to distinguish between the natural and the divine, for the divine is only a sublimated level of the natural.[6] This fails to see the spirit as an active and free reality that is not a necessitative substance. It is removed from life, conditioned by a naturalistic, rational, metaphysics and is, therefore, false.

True philosophy cannot be independent of the spirit, for it is of life. Knowledge is the activity of the spirit, which disallows relativism. Abstract thought is erroneous. Fundamental to this is "a phenomenology of the spiritual life." Basic is the distinction between the psychical and physical. Man is involved in both, but it is "only by the action of grace that he becomes a spiritual being," says Berdyaev. Thomism errs in either naturalizing grace or objectifying it.

"The first and most elementary point which must be established if there is to be any understanding of spirit is the distinction between 'spirit' and 'soul.' Soul belongs to nature, and its reality is of the natural order, for it is not less natural than body."[7] Yet the soul is not the same as body or matter, nor does the spirit oppose them as though recognized only in or by God. It is "from the depths" that spirit embraces body, matter and soul while belonging to another order of reality. Nature is illuminated by spirit, and soul does not imply their separation. Spirit is not an objective substance; it is life including experience and destiny through which it is known. Spirit is basic to the knowing subject even as it is also known. All that is real in the spiritual realm is so through the knowing subject, yet the knowing subject is not alien to what is objective to its consciousness.[8] This adds up to a phenomenological perspective.

"Spiritual life is the most real kind of life," says Berdyaev. Not objective, neither is it purely subjective. This implies a phenomenology, which interrelates consciousness with physical perceptions without their correspondence to our ideas. The spirit is real but not objectively provable. The divine is manifested in spiritual experience but cannot be demonstrated in any form of ratiocination. There is "no proof that my own spiritual life does not exist," says Berdyaev. It is a manifestation of the spiritual world, which is self-authenticating. Those who claim that this amounts to auto-suggestion only reflect its absence in their own lives. It is a naturalistic tendency to deny spiritual experience, and it is usually an accompaniment of a bourgeois self-sufficiency.[9]

Positivism is an erroneous notion which proves ignorant of spiritual experience, since it relies solely upon scientific objectivity. Spiritual experience, unlike science, has an affinity between the knowing subject and the object. Spirit is transcendent of soul within the self as well as a metaphysical substance and objective reality. God cannot be substance, for God is spirit, which is like mobile energy, since spirit is Heraclitean, not Parmenidean. Similarly, personality is not substance, for it is dynamic spiritual energy and activity or creativity. It is personal and yet supra-personal. Spirit is liberty; not the bondage of nature, it makes for inner unity and destiny. It enlightens and transfigures the world through persons. The exterior material realities of history symbolize spirit as a spirituality. Psychology cannot coalesce with this philosophy of spirit. Descartes' dualism does not give it a favorable starting point, but Berdyaev believes that the spiritual life of mankind in history provides it "an indispensable premiss," and Sobornost is beyond both psychology and metaphysics, since it is linked with a concrete spiritual life of dedicated saints. It is beyond all abstract deductions.[10]

Hence, religion is deemed a life of the soul awakened to its intimacy with being through spiritual experience. In the life of the senses and the soul there is an isolation from being. Yet this does not imply that spiritual life is one of perfection free from sin. It can even fall away from its true nature. But by its faith the new Adam in Christ restores the fallen human nature.

Berdyaev declares that these occurrences in the spiritual world are reflected symbolically in the natural world. Erroneous theologians have placed creation solely within time and made it objective within the natural order. But Berdyaev specifies that "the Fall could not have taken place in the natural world, because this world is itself the result of the Fall." The Fall is an event in the spiritual world and is anterior to the world, occurring before time began as we know it. Hence it is wrong to translate Christian teachings and events into reason and nature, for God is "life" and cannot be expressed by categories of the natural world, including "the supernatural" so closely related. The language of spiritual experience is essential since symbolical of events. Even the ideas of soul and spirit are of mythological origin and are not of the natural world.[11]

Berdyaev sees that to demand criteria of revelation's authority is to seek support for God from the lower world of nature and thereby to enslave the spiritual to the natural. Any authoritarian approach does this, for it constrains rather than liberates. Barth's Calvinism goes wrong in a similar manner as do the doctrines of papal infallibility and Kant's ethical gnoseology. Each of these tries to be a criterion of truth apart from its spiritual possession; the same for the doctrines of biblical infallibility and naturalism. These notions pose as types of authoritarianism rather than as spiritual experience which allows God to be the sole authority and criterion of his truth. Often the church of history has been weakened by these trends by not amply correlating spirit and soul.[12] Berdyaev warns the church not to simply satisfy an intellectual curiosity lest we be led by its faults to a skepticism or agnosticism. True faith is an experience in the spirit, so we must not try to explain the higher in terms of the lower, yet the spiritual need not be separated from the psychical, moral and natural levels, but it must illuminate them.[13]

For Berdyaev the spirit is an important aspect of man who was created *imago dei*. He sees how extreme dualism is harmful. Sin distorts the divine image, for it is alien to spirit. Yet sinful man can be spiritually regenerated. We are born originally as the children of the first Adam, but this second birth is that by which we are made children of the second Adam, the "head of spiritual humanity" which lives on a deeper "interior level," says Berdyaev. This second birth is necessary and available to every Christian through their faith commitment to

Christ which enables them to be born again of the Spirit. In this context Berdyaev asserts that Christianity is the highest revelation of the spiritual life. Redemption is a mystery. "Calvary is an interior moment of life and of spiritual development, the submission of all life to crucifixion and to sacrifice." It is based on Agape or the Christ revealed self-giving love of God. Without the inward and spiritual acceptance of Christ, the truths of the Gospel remain unintelligible events and experiences. Gospel history is a meta-history; the spiritual plane is reflected, even mythologically, on the natural plane, where it is illuminated by the spirit symbolically.[14]

The spiritual life is a "qualitative unity" revealed in this life and reflects both the natures of God and man. Either of the two natures without the other would not make for vital spiritual life. Divine being must penetrate the being of man. In so doing it must "exteriorize itself" to make the encounter and penetration. Christian revelation is that of the spiritual life of being and is not an abstraction. Duns Scotus was one of the first thinkers who saw metaphysical arguments failing to grasp the spiritual mysteries.

Human personality is immortal but not because the soul is a metaphysical substance but rather is an experience of eternal life which is divinely human through Christ, the source of its life. Immortality is not an innate capacity but a gift-like acquisition of the spiritual birth and life in Christ, the source of eternal life. It is this higher quality of life which is eternal and that conquers death. Christ's resurrection gives assurance of this. Christianity, then, is not naturalistic. The paradox of the unity and duality of the divine and the human is at the heart of true spirituality. It is based on the God-man mystery of the incarnate Christ, which restores spirit to man. By this man is no longer "a self-contained, psycho-corporeal, monad," for he is transfigured, and only spiritual life can express the mystery of the resurrection of the flesh. Paradise is the return to a union of man, God and the cosmos. This reunion is living reality, it is life not merely inert substance.[15] "When man lost paradise it meant his separation from the cosmos and from the divine nature. . ." says Berdyaev. But restoration to unity remained possible within a cosmic consummation in the spiritual life of God's kingdom. It begins in the experience of love and beauty, not inert material substances.

Sometimes the historical church has reduced the Spirit to mere instruments, thus confusing ends with means, often with their hardened or objectivized symbols. Catholic sacramentalism reflects this. It obscures the new type of symbolism needed for a new spirituality. Berdyaev actually states that the destiny of Christianity depends upon this new spirituality. Either a new epoch with a Christian renaissance will come about or Christianity is doomed to perish, he says, while this will not likely happen, since "the gates of hell shall not prevail against it," as Jesus put it. Human dignity must be restored by the new spirituality accompanying the restored divine image in man. "God," says Berdyaev, "is immanent in spirit, but He transcends psycho-corporeal man and the natural world."[16] His quality supercedes man's quantities.

The Holy Spirit is infinite. He is where the divine and the human are united even in cultural expressions with possibilities for transfiguration of the cultural world. All intellectual, moral, artistic life and fellowship in love can be made more fruitful. Though in the church the doctrine of the Holy Spirit may be less prominent than the other persons of the Trinity, the Spirit is closer to man than they are, thinks Berdyaev, for the Spirit reveals new birth in the highest form of spiritual life which supercedes all custom, codes, collectivism and symbols. The Holy Spirit can liberate us from slavery to such things. Platonic thinking among the Patristic thinkers in this respect is superior to the Aristotelian, for it is closer to divine grace i.e. it is less stilted, constrained and confining.[17]

The Logos of the spiritual world is reflected symbolically in the natural world, giving it meaning. Symbols convey meaning dynamically and supra-rationally. "Our age," says Berdyaev, "has lost the meaning of things." The knowing subject is too often detached from the spiritual sources of life. Idealistic symbolism too often is reduced to subjectivism as fostered, for example, by Schleiermacher reducing religious truth to subjective values. Critically speaking this keeps man all wrapped up in himself. Subjective idealism fails to yield the dynamism of spiritual life. The divine is subjugated to what is transitory as related to outward forms and customs, and thus the spirit is quenched.[18] A symbol does not subject the infinite to the finite, though it allows the finite to be transparent to the infinite and thus transfuses divine energy into the world.

To separate the divine world from the human, as do both subjective and objective idealisms, tends to split the human spirit. But to identify the divine with the natural is a form of objectification and "denial of the mystery and infinitude of God's Being," says Berdyaev. Only symbols can penetrate and convey the meaning of God's being, for divinity is beyond rational concepts. Logos is not reducible to logic. The divine and the natural do not coalesce.[19] Faith is more than subjective insight such as that of Kant. Its principle symbolism opens up higher ways of knowledge and safeguards the distinctiveness of religious life, which regards God to be superior to what is either natural or rational. Much like Kierkegaard at this point, Berdyaev concedes an abyss between the infinite and the finite. Hence, it takes myth to bring us to the divine-within-the natural. We need not be ashamed of Christian mythology, including Adam and Eve and the fall, for it expresses what reason cannot. Similarly, the Trinity can be a symbol giving warmly meaningful hints to us where rational doctrines thereof remain harsh or cold. By it reason is illuminated uniquely through Christ; its doctrinal concepts are almost abandoned in favor of symbolic thought.[20]

Rational knowledge of God is to be deemed impossible, yet religious philosophy of the divine is not. When reason is enlightened by the spirit, even through symbols, it can affirm religious knowledge by being raised to a higher level than the natural or rational. Symbols supercede words and concepts. Symbols are important when they lead men to the Kingdom of God and to union between God and men. They help man attain the transfiguration of life as they point to how spirit transcends man while regenerating him in existence.[21] Thus they help open up a vital relation to eternity from within time.[22]

Notes

1. F. R. Barry, *Recovery of Men*, Chapter V, pp. 78–85.

2. *Ibid.*

3. Berdyaev, *Freedom and the Spirit*, pp. vii to x.

4. *Ibid*, pp. x to xv.

5. *Ibid*, pp. xviv-xx; Chapter I.

6. *Ibid*, pp. 1–3.

7. *Ibid*, p. 8. Cf. pp. 4–7.

8. *Ibid*, pp. 7–9.

9. *Ibid*, pp. 11–14.

10. *Ibid*, pp. 15–20. The term "Saints" here is used in the N.T. sense, not as in either historical theology or popular thought.

11. *Ibid*, pp. 21–26.

12. *Ibid*, p. 27.

13. *Ibid*, p. 28.

14. *Ibid*, pp. 28–36.

15. *Ibid*, pp. 37–42.

16. *Ibid*, p. 47. Cf. pp. 40–47.

17. *Ibid*, pp. 47–51.

18. *Ibid*, pp. 52–58; 60–62.

19. *Ibid*, pp. 62–66.

20. *Ibid*, pp. 67–68; 69–74f.

21. *Ibid*, pp. 81–85.

22. Cf. Slaatte, *Time, Existence and Destiny*, Peter Lang, Inc. N.Y., Berlin et al.

Chapter IV

Personality and Creativity

In his notable early book *Der Sinn des Schaffens* Berdyaev states, "The creative act is always liberation and victory. It is the experience of power." This is not merely a matter of emotional exclamation. Only he who has been liberated from egocentricism and selfish ambition is strong enough to be "a creator and personality," says Berdyaev. When this is realized there is a "birth of God in man" through God-manhood. The human creativity involved justifies man as man.[1]

Philosophy is more than a science, for it is an act of creativity, since it is a moral, aesthetic and religious art, an art of knowledge in freedom which creates new ideas. Values become important as new ideas for finding meaning in the world. "Intuition," says Berdyaev, "is the ultimate in philosophy,—logic the penultimate."[2] Akin to Bergson here, Berdyaev sees how creative philosophy expels the domination of scientific necessity. Intuition is basic and fosters the comprehension of things.[3]

Creativeness is inspired by the Holy Spirit related to man's redemption unto a new creation whereby man is made into a new Adam. "Christ would not be God-man if human nature were passive or bound, and nothing out of itself would be disclosed. . . . Revelation in this respect is not only divine but also preeminently human."[4]

"But real creativity is possible only through redemption," says Berdyaev. "In the act of the redemption from sin the conventional moral moment will be mystically transformed, and through Love and Grace be transfigured."[5] Creativeness is *for* something while it presupposes redemption *from* something, viz evil.[6] Nietzsche did not know that the religion of redemption and the religion of creativity were one and the same. Like many people he failed to observe the ascent from law to redemption (Erlösing) to creativity (Schaffens).[7]

In *Le Sens de l'acte createur*[8] Berdyaev begins the theme of creation in terms of "the creative vocation of man" viewed inwardly and biographically. He asserts that creative activity has no need of justification; it rather justifies man as linked with the God-man and its relation to culture.

"Man" says Berdyaev, "is justified not only by his docility before a supreme power but also by his creative exaltation." The creative act is for him neither a demand nor a human right but a command of God addressed to man as an ultimate obligation." God respects the creative act of man in response to the creative act of God. It inspires regard for freedom and equality as derived from creation. God reclaims the freedom of man, which is a duty of man from man's regard for God. But Berdyaev asserts that "God cannot reveal to man unless man is willing to be open to God."[9]

Creativity is fundamental to the divine-human principle of activated Christianity. "Man expects the birth of God in him. God expects the birth of him in man." (and) "The thought that God has need of man, of his response and of his creativity is a thought singularly audacious, but without the audacity the revelation of man-God would be deprived of meaning."[10] Berdyaev states, "The divine drama is counterparted in the human drama and is known in spiritual experience and theological speculation." Implied in this is a loving God, which would be impossible without someone to love. A rational concept cannot do justice to this; it calls for spiritual symbolism and commitment. "The mystery of creation is counterparted in the mystery of redemption as another dramatic act of spiritual activity," says Berdyaev. Here a rational ontology is displaced by a "phenomenology of spiritual experience" expressed symbolically. It is in itself an ecstasy which opens up to the infinite. Yet a tragic element enters at this point through a disproportion between the creative design and its realization. For Berdyaev the problem is not a sanctification of the cosmos but a spiritual meaning through a new religious authropology; not a naturalistic type while different from that of both the early fathers and the Scholastics, it relates to the existential struggle of conscience and the consciousness of sin.[11] Here meet the contrasting poles of human existence, creation and redemption.

Berdyaev states that he has always been an existentialist type of thinker. He regards as his best book *The Destiny of Man* written much later than *The Meaning of Creativity*, which came out of his earlier storm and stress period.[12] To blend his spiritual metaphysics with theology, Berdyaev espoused the existential perspective in his Existenzphilosophie. It allows man to be seen on more than the natural and empirical levels. Thus Berdyaev became a disciple of Kierkegaard but a balanced type of existentialist embracing a critical realism.

Creation presupposes freedom, not in being as such but in "neant" or the meonic not-being of ex nihilo, cosmic freedom, which is even presupposed by God's creativeness. "The creative acts of man have a need for matter and cannot be surpassed by the reality of the world. . . But the creative acts cannot be entirely determined by the material of the world." The element of freedom is inherent in all creation and creativity. In this respect creation is *ex nihilo* and the problem of how the non-existent becomes existent remains a mystery.[13] Even so it involves freedom as the cosmic or meonic freedom which is presupposed by moral and spiritual freedom including divine creation.

Berdyaev has a dynamic philosophy because of his Christian theosophy, which is much like that of such early church fathers as Clement of Alexandria, Origen, St. Gregory of Nyssa, Cardinal Nicholas of Cusa and later mystical thinkers like Jacob Boehme, St. Martin, Francis Baader and Vladimir Soloviev. Similar to their perspectives he still sees differences in Christian anthropologies. Catholic theology, he contends, views man as having lost his "supernatural gifts" through the fall, and he may recover them only by a special gift of grace. On this basis human nature is interpreted naturalistically, for Thomism regards natural man as "a non-spiritual being," says Berdyaev. He declares that in Protestant theology the Fall has completely distorted human nature and deprived man of freedom and made all his life dependent on grace. This view is a Barthian interpretation that is prone to belittle man. The Orthodox view of man places emphasis upon the divine image and likeness in man as a spiritual being. Wesleyan theology is closer to this.

But, critically, Berdyaev is seemingly unaware of the various views of anthropology in Protestant circles. For example, the Arminian to Wesleyan view of man's nature as reflecting the free will in man to respond to the initiative of God's grace; this keeps man addressable and salvageable while grace-dependent. Despite the fall he is still man, a sinful man at that, while the *imago dei* is not totally obliterated, lest man not be man.

Berdyaev rejects the stilted Thomistic concept of God as *actus purus*, which deprives God of a dynamic inner vitality and power. He states that the deism of the Enlightenment, presupposed by modern atheisms, is a consequence of Aristotelian thinking, for, he says, ". . . a lifeless object of speculation must ultimately disintegrate faith" even as it reduces all modes of cognition to rationalisms which lead to skepticism and agnosticism.[14] Berdyaev could see how Thomism was enslaved to a naturalistic metaphysics that minimized the spiritual kind. It views the "supernatural" or divine as merely a higher form of the natural. St. Bonaventure had already seen this weakness. Berdyaev could also see how the naturalistic metaphysics of Aristotle and Thomas Aquinas was seen to be "irreconcilable with an autonomous doctrine of the Spirit and *a fortiori* with theology as the wisdom of the divine Spirit."[15] A parallel in modern Protestant theology of the past century reflects how preoccupation with empirical naturalism leads to the neglect of the Holy Spirit's important role.[16] Berdyaev creatively extends this criticism in *Solitude and Society* and in *Slavery and Freedom* to all metaphysics from Aquinas to German idealism. He contends that idealism delivered man from being reduced to an object, but at the same time it interpreted the subject in an objective manner. The subject was treated as an object especially in Hegel's philosophy. The human personality was submerged rationally in the Absolute System of Cosmic Being.

For Berdyaev genuine theology is apophatic or a direct mystical appropriation of truth rather than cataphatic or a matter of rationalistic cognition; the weakness of the latter is the inability of reason to mediate ultimate truths. In this respect Berdyaev has much in common with John Wesley's emphasis upon the Spirit-with-spirit experience of the Holy Spirit. It is an inward personal realization, not an outward doctrinal or sacerdotal imposition. Berdyaev is profoundly personal and doctrinaire in his mystical theology looking to Jacob Boehme and back to Plotinus.[17] In this light Berdyaev appreciates Soloviev's place for God-manhood but looks eschatologically to a spiritual transformation of all men with *theosis* as the ultimate mission of the church while not based absolutely upon a priestly hierarchy either papal or imperial.[18]

The freedom of spirit is what distinguishes the concrete being of personality from the abstract being of metaphysics, especially rationalistic metaphysics. Freedom of spirit is anterior to being. But since man to Berdyaev is the co-creator of God within history, man's freedom which is basic to his creativeness, must be "uncreated" in the sense of being linked with the "meonic freedom" presumed in God's creativeness. Berdyaev holds to this with support from Boehme's view of *Ungrund*; God is co-existent with freedom, though this is a mystery which remains unexplained.

It is fair to say that Berdyaev has a "religious philosophy," not just a "philosophy of religion." This is because he sees the knowing process is not removed from religious experience any more than any other experience. Knowledge is in itself a dynamic process of religious significance. One does not philosophize about religion as something objectively removed from the knowing process, for knowledge is integral to existence as is religion itself. The philosopher cannot rationally project himself outside his religion to examine it but must see it from within. Nor can he do justice to this spiritual apprehension through objective concepts assumed to be equal to Being as in naive realism. The philosopher is existentially oriented and cannot pretend to be otherwise; hence, his scheme of thought, even focused on religion in relation to the universe, must be existentially oriented. In short, Berdyaev's is a religious philosophy because his is a religious existence, which inspires creative thought.

Greek categories of thought do not make it possible to do justice to a dynamic, holistic existence. The Christian revelation with its strong idea of personality gives both new content and higher dimension to thought. Personality is not a natural phenomenon, says Berdyaev, nor a datum of the "objective world," for it is the image of God, and here lies its sole claim to existence. It is because of this that knowledge belongs to the destiny of personality.[19] The Christian Gospel places "the ontological kernel of the human personality in "the heart," which really is "the integral whole" of the personality, as Berdyaev claims. The heart is also the creative seat of man's philosophical understanding, wisdom and conscience in a way that reason is not. Here Berdyaev is closely akin to Pascal, who saw *esprit de finesse* more basic to knowledge than *esprit de geometrie* and could say, "The heart has reasons that reason knows not of."[20] The heart to Berdyaev is "the supreme organ of evaluation."[21] In a similar vein, intuition is a spiritual creative capacity of the human personality essential to knowledge. Personality, then, is "extra-natural" having a relation to God and "a consciousness of its unity in the midst of change."[22] It is not a part but a whole and never a mere natural phenomenon but is "a datum of the inner world of existence."[23] Religion deals with the realization of the divine purpose of personality. Berdyaev so views this as to make it possible to say that his existentialism is what protects personalism from rationalism.[24]

Again, Berdyaev's is a creatively religious philosophy, because he regards philosophical thought as belonging to concrete experience as a "function of life." It is a symbol and expression of man's spiritual experience, for man is spirit. Berdyaev states, "Philosophy cannot ever be divorced from the totality of man's spiritual experience, from his struggles, his insights, his ecstasies, his religious faith and mystical vision."[25] Philosophy springs from the very person of existence who creatively reflects and ponders things; it is not a mere part of him like reason nor is it of an abstract mind or subject removed from concrete existence. Furthermore, a Christian philosopher cannot rightly philosophize and remain unaffected by his doctrinal convictions; therefore, his philosophical reflection must be creatively Christian in both its existential orientation and outcome.

May we let Berdyaev himself provide us with a summary of what we describe as his religious philosophy over against either a philosophy of religion or a systematic theology. He says, "I can only admit a phenomenology which describes metaphysical reality in symbolic terms. Any rationalization of the di-vine-human relationship, attempt at expressing it in terms of a rational philosophy of being, makes nonsense both of that re-lationship and of that philosophy."[26]

Notes

1. Berdyaev, *Der Sinn des Schaffens*, English translation, pp. 3–11. The French title is *Le Sens de l'acte createur.* referred to below.

2. *Ibid*, pp. 13–30, 31. (German)

3. *Ibid*, pp. 31–33.

4. *Ibid*, p. 99.

5. *Ibid*, pp.101, 104.

6. *Ibid*, pp 104, 106.

7. *Ibid*, p. 106f.

8. *Esprit*, August, 1948, pp. 179–191.

9. *Ibid*, p. 180.

10. *Ibid*, p. 180.

11. *Ibid*, p. 181.

12. *Ibid*, pp. 181–183.

13. *Ibid*, pp. 184ff.

14. Berdyaev, *Freedom and the Spirit*, Introduction. Cf. Edgar Munzer *Univ. of Toronto Quarterly*, Vol 14, 1945, p. 188ff, 192.

15. Munzer, *op cit*, p. 191.

16. This is confirmed by the writings of theologians like Sangster, Charles Williams and Dillistone. CF. my forthcoming book, "Modern and Contemporary Theologies," Univ. Press of Am., 1997.

17. Munzer, *op cit*, p. 190f.

18. *Ibid*, p. 191.

19. *Solitude And Society*, pp. 132, 128.

20. Pascal, *Pensees*

21. *Solitude And Society*, p. 128.

22. *Ibid*, p. 122.

23. *Ibid*, p. 133.

24. Quite opposed to Edgar S. Brightman's Hegelian personalism.

25. *Dream and Reality*, p. 104.

26. *Ibid*, p. 209.

Chapter V

Personality and Existence

Epistemologically, Berdyaev saw the superiority of the subject over the object. The object is dependent upon the knowing subject and is phenomenalistic, because it is a product of the interpretations of the combined sensate and rational insights of the knowing subject. Truth and meaning are subjective, not objective; the subject conceives the object and/or its meaning. Knowledge, then, is not passive but creative, for it is of the knowing subject, who as personality belongs to everyday existence.

Creativity is the clue to conquering one's enslavement to objectification, objectivity and materialism. It is enhanced by the return to God in spiritual communion. Religious help toward this is regeneration and charismatic transformation. There can be no genuine community without a communion of persons. In this respect redeemed persons of faith can be of special help in strengthening the Kingdom of God. This implies an active and responsible salvation that is not self-centered while subjectively relevant and serviceable to the harmony of divine providence and eschatological fulfillment.[1]

Berdyaev's existential leanings are related to the selfhood and primacy of the knowing subject in concrete existence. This gives strength to the inner self and the consciousness basic to it. Emanuel Mounier, who respected this view, also saw how the opposite or positivistic thinking tends to distort and even negate the subject by treating it as "a synonym for unreality."

Like Berdyaev he saw that "a person is a spiritual being" who
has his "own responsible activity and freedom as well as creative acts." The personalisms of both Berdyaev and Mounier
affirm the absolute value of the person, and the person is not
to be viewed as a means but an end; it is an "incarnated self,"
as Mounier suggests.[2] Personality is basic.

Berdyaev's personalism is a philosophical expansion of what
is experienced by the self in his/her concrete daily existence.
This amounts to an existentialist perspective of both the self
and what it subjectively observes. As personality it provides
one with a close-to-home perspective of things, which sees the
subject-self as the core of reality and center of knowledge. Upon
examining the everyday problems of people this makes for
understanding things in relation to one's own selfhood and
inner being at the center of one's consciousness. Unexplain-
able in objective terms this inner selfhood or personality also
yields insight into the subjectivity of other persons. It is what
prophets and poets refer to as "the heart" and appertains to
the conscious-to-sub-conscious inwardness of the self essential
to everything from romance to religion. It is what the self per-
ceives inwardly and cannot be perceived outwardly; it is subjectivity as prior even to objectivity. It is what can say "I" or
"me" and know what that means whether definable or not.
Also, epistemologically speaking, Berdyaev saw that a rational
knowledge of what is irrational is impossible. This appertains
not only to emotional problems but such things as the will,
intuition and spirit of man. Knowledge is seen to be related
not only to being but to existential phenomena even disclosing the mysteries within being and concrete existence. Being,
then, is to be conceived as interior, not exterior. It emanates
from the self or concrete subject of existence. Whenever the
subject-self objectifies a concept it forms an object. This process is one of disintegration even as it reflects the fallen state
of man, the knower. Its pseudo-projections are unrealistic.
Realism, in fact, fails to take into account the phenomenological implications and the epistemological contributions of the
knowing subject.[3] The subject's projections are from within
the self; they are imperfect representations but must be taken
seriously, since they belong to the knowing self and cannot be
shunted aside.

Existential philosophy is based upon the personal existence of the self, who chooses himself, as Kierkegaard said. Even when one despairs it is because the self has not alienated himself from his thoughts and problems but has chosen himself. Also, the philosophical perspective is one of viewing things from his very own point-of-view. One encounters himself as he does so. This gives primacy to one's own indigenous consciousness in contrast to the world. It places one's subjective existence over against "the crowd" and what Heidegger calls *das Man*, the impersonal "one" and conventional view of man as "mass man."[4]

But existentially Kierkegaard moves beyond the choice of self, which eventuates in despair. He asks, "What does it mean to be a Christian?" Paradox enters the picture as the answer is seen to involve this: "He who would save his life must lose it," as Jesus said. Kierkegaard expands this in his *Sickness Unto Death* with anticipations in his *Either/Or* (Enten-Eller) and practical reflections in the *Journals*.[5] The choice of oneself eventually leads to despair, since one can neither evade himself nor become his true self apart from decisions, which establish his existence under God. Only when broken in self-sufficiency can one "choose himself before God." This is because sin emerges in the presence of God, and only our consciousness of sin can give us a critical point of view evoking our honesty and penitence. This is akin to Socrates' claim that "virtue is knowledge." Despair is overcome only through one's faith commitment. What to Augustine was "freedom minor" or moral freedom is now moved into "freedom major" or the freedom of choosing only the good with an undivided heart under God. To retain this true or major freedom is to give it back to God. As George Matheson wrote, "Make me a captive, Lord, and then I shall be free." When this paradox is realized, Kierkegaard's comment can be appreciated: "It takes moral courage to grieve, but it takes religious courage to rejoice."[6]

In this light God is not rational *ousia*, *essentia* or Being, but Subject-Spirit or the great 'I Am' of the Bible and is known as the ultimate Person-Self who is encountered faithwise and known only in that existential encounter, what S. K. called the "Moment." The relationship between God and man is of an "I-Thou" encounter of subjects and communion of faith. Objectification is an erroneous kind of epistemological theorizing in all fields, including religion. It catapults the knowing subject into a de-personalized world that obscures the subject-self or personality.

For a proper apprehension of Berdyaev's epistemology and philosophy in general it is important to assert that he repudiated the idea that realism and idealism are the only legitimate theories of knowledge. In contrast to these theories Berdyaev employs a third alternative, which alone he considers valid. It is the existential personalist epistemology. The realist, Berdyaev believes, tends to neglect the fact that the activity of the subject is not limited to thought but that the subject himself participates in being or that the knower is existential. "The subject himself is being—if we have to use this term—and the only authentic being is that of the subject," said Berdyaev.[7] The knowing subject, Berdyaev asserts, is also voluntarist. The will of man, besides his thought, plays a great role in knowledge. The subject creates things in the created world. "From the authentic existential standpoint reality is not a creation of knowledge, but knowledge is a creative art."[8] What is objective really depends on, and is the projection of, the subject. Idealism, whether absolute or subjective, is thought by Berdyaev to deny man's creative role as a knower. Consequently the creative subject is reduced to a general consciousness, which is not true to man as personality. Thus human creativity is made null and void.

As an existentialist Nicholas Berdyaev saw that the knowing subject is oriented rightly only when he dispenses with the rational process of objectification. The knower should not project his ideas into a supposed outside ontological realm which stands over against him. That which he apprehends is not an object but an aspect of his human existence. It is through this human existence that he can have dealings with the divine in whose image he was created. This epistemological principle is of consequence to Berdyaev's entire religious philosophy. It implies that a meaning is to be found which illuminates human existence from within as a "part of the Divine Being." God is the great "I AM" who, too, is a subject.

The crux of this is that in order for there to be a meaning to existence there must be the spiritual activity of the personal subject which involves "the integral rather than the partial reason."[9] Knowledge itself is a creative act of experience. It is human existence being given meaning so that Being as existence is illuminated, regenerated and enriched.[10] It means that the creative knowing subject or personality is participating in existence and Being. This is a spiritual process, for Being is dynamic and pneumatic. Knowledge belongs to a dynamic spirit-with-Spirit relationship between man and Being-in-existence.

Too often philosophers have settled for abstract systems which betray the concrete persons of daily existence. The existentialist view is no less than a plea for the overlooked person of everyday existence in contrast to the objectified versions of man as measured by tabulated aptitudes and achievements as well as statistical phenomena that can be causally explained away. It centers around the self as a personality rather than as a rational concept. Hegel's German idealism was an extreme case in point as it postulated an objective philosophy of universal reason, which overlooked the existential perspective of concrete persons, both the thinker himself and the persons he deals with.

But there remains the problem of the philosopher himself. Actually, the integral spiritual life of the philosopher as a man always precedes his philosophy and its epistemological grounds. Berdyaev states, "The mystery of existence can be regarded as the ultimate problem of philosophy." It is at the beginning and not the end of one's philosophizing. We should not pose the knowing subject and his knowledge as apart from each other. Before being became an object of knowledge "it was a subject of knowledge."[11] This involves the existential perspective and the primacy of the thinking self.

Existentialism stresses that the person is related to the primacy of existence. "Existence precedes essence," as Sartre puts it. This is contrary to all rationalisms from the classical philosophy of Plato and Aristotle through Descartes and Hegel as well as the modern realists like Whitehead. For Plato what to us is the realistic world of everyday life was only a shadow of his ideal world. The existential perspective of concrete existence implies the knowing subject, who is responsible for his destiny, because he is morally free. Existentialists declare that we are free in every respect but one i.e. we are "not free not to be free," as David Victoroff put it.[12] This total freedom is a total responsibility. As Dostoievsky declared, "We are all responsible for all." Berdyaev appreciated this.

The irrational elements in daily life or concrete existence are important while often incomprehensible. Christianity has concern for the plenitude of what is existent to the self. God deals with individual selves, not abstract concepts like the Ideas of Plato and Aristotle. As the great "I Am" God is the Absolute Spirit-self as personality or Spirit, not abstract being. Biblically this is maximized as personality in the Incarnation. (Cf. Exodus 3:14 and II Corinthians 5:19). It is the great "I Am" or Yahweh encountered by Moses and other prophets. In the light of "God was in Christ. . ." it comes to its crescendo in Jesus Christ as the God-man.

Man's essence is not found in his existence. Man has not finalized anything as long as he exists in this mundane temporal world. Hence the Christian existentialist knows of the anguish or Dread which Kierkegaard stresses, and he understands the inner tortures of Pascal. The atheistic existentialist deprives himself of God and is left to concoct his own ethical values. "But," as Victoroff says, "whereas for the (atheistic) existentialist man's very existence in the world is incomprehensible, gratuitous, in the last resort simply absurd, Christianity gives an aim to human life, and, in so doing, does away with this ultimate absurdity."[13] —an absurdity intensified by so much relativism in the modern intellectual world and everyday life.

A major antidote to this relativism and absurdity is faith in the divine Absolute of God-in-Christ and his dynamic love ethics, which keeps subjectivity superior to objectivity.

Notes

1. See my previous book, *Time, Existence and Destiny*, Peter Lang Pub. Co., NY, 1988.

2. Emmaniel Mounier, *A Personalist Manifesto*, Longmans, Green and Co., London, 1938, pp. 78f; 67–79ff.

3. Berdyaev, *Spirit and Reality*. pp. 8–10, 31.

4. Emmet, Dorothy M., "Kierkegaard and the Existential Philosophy," *Philosophy*, Vol. XVI, 1946, London, MacMillan and Co., Ltd. pp. 257, 260, 262.

5. *Ibid*, pp. 263ff.

6. Soren Kierkegaard, *Journals*, 343.

7. *Spirit and Reality*, p. 8.

8. *Ibid*.

9. *Solitude and Society*, p. 53.

10. *Ibid*.

11. Berdiaeff, "Le philosophe et l'existence," Actualite's scientifique et industrielles, (533), IV, pp. 43–50, esp. 43–45.

12. David Victoroff, "The Christian Sources of Existentialism, "*Sobornost*, Series 3, no. 3, Summer, 1948, p. 82.

13. *Ibid*, p. 84, cf. pp. 81–84.

PART TWO

SPIRIT AND ETHICAL ISSUES

Chapter VI

Ethics and Its Types

Berdyaev indicated that there are three basic types of ethics.
Though often interrelated in existence, they are differentiable
by distinctive features or qualities. The three types of ethics
are: legalistic ethics, redemptive ethics and creative ethics. The
present discussion will appertain to each and all of these ethical types.

Legalistic ethics places the premium on law and its interpretation. Legalistic moralism tends to condemn people, so it
is often immoral from the standpoint of higher types of ethics. Asceticism tends to err because of its implicit legalism,
though it is less likely to err when mystically based. Yet laws
are essential, because of a sinful society; therefore, they cannot be cancelled.

Normative ethics is legalistic and caters to Pharisaism.
Kantian systems of idealism promote this legalistically, though
it tries to remain autonomous. Since Kant's ethics makes every
person morally authoritative, it makes them ends rather than
means. Yet they are instruments of universal law. As such their
autonomy is questionable, since they are subservient to law. In
this respect the emotional side of moral life is minimized, if
not denied, by Kant.[1]

Tolstoy legalistically regarded the Gospel as based on moral
norms and laws and was close to a Pelagian self-sufficiency
without grace. Yet as Lutheranism attacked it, it, too, became
legalistic. From a legalistic perspective a person becomes good
by his good works, but in truth a man does good works be-

cause he is good. Yet this matter of being good must come from spiritual re-motivation, not merely self concern. As Berdyaev states it, "The Gospel transcends and cancels the ethics of law, replacing it by a different and higher ethics of love and freedom."[2] Even so the law teaches principles even to redeemed persons. Christians live by both grace and law. Grace redeems and re-motivates men, but law specifies righteous conduct in society.

Law serves to protect personal freedom. But human life cannot wait for the perfect regeneration of society; meanwhile law makes life in general more tolerable than otherwise. In this respect Grace and law are correlative. Thus Grace sublimates law without rejecting it. Law promotes happiness largely through human respect and obedience.[3] Yet grace is often legalistically misinterpreted as in Roman Catholic piety which minimizes justification by faith. It is commonly supported by psychologies which foster happiness, whereas existential thinkers like Dostoevsky, Nietzsche and Kierkegaard disproved such rationalistic and hedonistic doctrine. Berdyaev says men prefer spiritual freedom and creativeness to happiness.[4] To seek happiness directly is often to miss it.

Law does not change human nature or remotivate it. But redemption frees men from fear of the law's powers. It unites the good with everyday existence, "bridging the gulf made by the law as a consequence of sin. . ." It destroys the roots of sin and evil, and thereby frees man from the absolute power of the law. Redemption means, first and foremost, liberation. "The Redeemer is the Liberator."[5]

Redemption also means "a revolutionary change in moral valuations" as Berdyaev expresses it. Redemptive ethics means that the moral act is done in collaboration with God's love. But to be realized the act must be inspired by commitment to Christ, yet this cannot be done morally alone but redemptively under Grace. Christianity is above the ideas of supreme good and our own ideas of the good. It is not based upon an idealistic abstraction but upon a divine Personality and the God and man relationship. Gospel ethics is not based upon abstract moralisms or ideals. It is centered in concrete existence and not dependent upon projected laws or norms. Hence, the Sabbath is made for man, not man for the Sabbath. Spirit is placed before law. Every moral problem for the Christian demands its own solution; the person involved is prior to the norm or law being considered. It must be "based upon the greatest possible consideration for the man from whom it procedes and for the man upon whom it is directed." This is existential in nature, not idealistic. Kant's law of universality is to be questioned. The uniqueness of the moral act itself and its situation must be respected; thus individual cases must be respected over intellectual or social universals.[6]

Redemptive ethics is the ethics of love, which cannot be focused upon an abstract norm or law but must be focused upon the person that it looks to. Love for God is also love for a person, not merely a principle. Christian love then is personal; humanistic love is impersonal. Erroneously, humanism places the welfare of mankind ahead of the person. When good works are used to express one's love for God they represent a false view of the Gospel. True love seeks no reward; it is its own reward. It regards each person as of the highest value and worth more than the world. Persons should not be comparatively judged. The only impurity is that of the heart. "To be strict to oneself and kind to others—this is the truly Christian attitude," says Berdyaev. The Gospel equalizes us before God, whether righteous or unrighteous. The imago dei is seen in every person and implies possibilities in each and all of us.

Christian morality is redemptive and is to be viewed as the morality of strength. Nietzsche failed to understand this thinking in terms of "slave morality." Not slavish, Christian ethics is for the strong in spirit, not the weak; Christ is the key here. Humility, is not weakness but a manifestation of spiritual power in the conquest of all fear including fear of death. It is also basic to overcoming egocentric selfhood.[7] Paradoxically, Christianity sees persons as bearing the imago dei; even if they are wicked. It promotes the love for all including the sinful. Though salvation is offered to everyone the exclusive concern for only one's own soul is satanic.[8] Christians should first think of the needs of others.

The ethics of law tends to destroy rather than save, for it is pitiless and without Grace. Christian ethics is redemptive and much concerned about the sufferings of others. It is possible only because it is divinely human through Christ, the God-man. The Gospel teaches us not to fear suffering despite its evil; even God in the Son suffered. Other religions are afraid of suffering and seek to avoid it, Buddhism and Stoicism being conspicuous cases in point. Christianity faces up to suffering and finds it meaningful through the Cross. Suffering is bitter only when we refuse it. Accepting it under Grace is redemptive. This does not imply that we should endorse all sufferings, especially the products of injustice. Influenced by Dostoevsky's *Brothers Karamazov* Berdyaev writes, "At the same time pity is the strongest proof of man's belonging to a higher world."[9] Ascetic attitudes do not promote such. I'm reminded of a well-fixed man who moved outside an intervening section of the worst types of homes I had ever seen. "What do you do when you drive through that section of town?" I asked. He replied, "I look the other way."

Often attitudes would become more Christian if we regarded all persons as though they were dying, suggests Berdyaev. Yet he says every person is dying, so why not be compassionate toward him? Christ is in the present, said Kierkegaard. He is our "eternal contemporary," so he liberates us now and makes possible under Grace what is not possible under the law, namely sacrificial love. Hence the Gospel is the most radical revolution of values in history. It makes love not merely an ideal but an experience.[10]

The ethics of creativeness is an activated expansion of redemptive ethics. Basic is the use of one's talents with a sense of vocation. Creativeness is bringing about something new or something out of nothing or non-being. By it nothing becomes something. Berdyaev declares that "true creativeness always involves catharsis, purification, liberation of the spirit from psycho-physical elements and victory over them."[11] Creativeness presupposes meonic freedom, the cosmic freedom basic to creation and creativity; creating out "of nothing" is one type of freedom.[12] Creative activity can help one forget himself and work for others. It is not only a personal right but is a duty. It is involved, too, in the creation of values and is not restricted to stated norms the way the ethics of law is. Law yields but finite ethics. Ethical creativeness is infinite. Yet it is not limited to redemptive ethics since inspired to be more than individualistic. Even redemptive ethics is prone to be individualistic about salvation. The ethics of creativeness moves beyond the concern for personal salvation with concern for righteousness and its applied values. It is apt to be quite selfless. Thinkers who have contributed the most to the ethics of creativeness are the religious existentialists previously mentioned. This kind of ethics is not altogether individualistic but is personalistic. To be one's true self is to be like God's idea of your true self, a personal bearer of the divine principles of life in God's image.[13]

The ethics of creativeness is not passive but active and seeks to improve the world. Religiously it strives for the victory of eternity over time as it is directed to eternal values, truth, righteousness and beauty.[14] Creative ethics ascends to the divine. It has a spiritual force or "fire", says Berdyaev, which overcomes evil passions. Positive in nature it is transformed into something higher than negative prohibitions. Virtues need this dynamic quality, lest they dry up; passions must be sublimated and transformed, sex being the most likely passion to fall.[15] Redemptive ethics blended with creative ethics does not condone the person who disregards moral law. Creativeness includes sacrifice and yields happiness. It is a matter of freedom and is unlike herd morality or social conformity. Creative imagination plays an important role here, as it envisions and images a better life. God created through imagination, says Berdyaev. Hence, the fuller creative ethics must be one of freedom, compassion and creativeness.[16] Redemptive ethics blesses creative ethics unto a fuller fulfillment.

Human conscience is a significant capacity, a divine gift of creation. It is not a social accruement. If it were it would be reduced to total relativism and lack inner authority. Berdyaev brings this out in his essay, "The Critique of Pure Conscience" in which he attacks Kant's idealistic view. He does not align his ethics fully with Kant, for a finite reason, even moral in nature, cannot do justice to the infinite or the absolute. Yet conscience is to be respected as a person's moral voice, even if imperfect, for it is still connected with God through the imago dei. The strength of conscience lies in its ties with both freedom and grace, because it was not irreparably damaged by the fall. It is man's meeting point of the two worlds or orders of existence, the divine and the human.[17] This ethical position has much in common with John Wesley's theory of "prevenient Grace" or the divine factors which function even before one accepts saving Grace.

Religious legalism creates distinctive fears. It also creates the distinction between the sacred and the profane and often elicits fear of the sacred. But fear is vitiated with a sense of sin, from which only the Gospel liberates people. The expression "fear of God" should be replaced by "reverence/awe for God," as this writer claims in a Berdyaev-like manner. The word *fear* in religion is often an old English word, which is misleading.

Agape love is not abstract but particular and personal. Its true purpose is "to reach union of souls, fellowship, and brotherhood."[18] It cannot be neutral or be an "even-up" sharing with everyone without distinction. It is individualistic basically while social in outreach.[19] Spiritual or redemptive love is not meant to denounce natural love but to transfigure and enlighten it. Love for persons should not be sacrificed to love of principles or ideals or utopias. To love abstractions is idolatrous. "Compassion means union in suffering, while love may be union in joy and bliss," says Berdyaev.[20] The most mature Christian love is redemptive in spirit and motive; therefore, it is also creative and outgoing in its activated sacrifice and service. Thus, expressed Agape love is the highest form of Christian witness and ethical fulfillment.

Notes

1. Berdyaev, *The Destiny of Man*, pp. 95–98.

2. *Ibid*, p. 99.

3. *Ibid*, p. 100–102.

4. *Ibid*, p. 103.

5. *Ibid*, p. 104.

6. *Ibid*, p. 105–107.

7. *Ibid*, pp. 107–108.

8. *Ibid*, pp. 108–114.

9. *Ibid*, p. 120, 115–119.

10. *Ibid*, p. 120–124.

11. *Ibid*, p. 126.

12. *Ibid*, pp. 124–128.

13. *Ibid*, pp. 130–135.

14. See my books: *Time And Its End* and *Time, Existence and Destiny*.

15. Berdyaev, *The Destiny of Man*, pp. 136–139.

16. *Ibid*, p. 140–143; 148–152.

17. *Ibid*, pp. 153–168.

18. *Ibid*, pp. 170–174.

19. *Ibid*, p. 177–187.

20. *Ibid*, p. 192.

Chapter VII

Ethics and Phenomenology

Berdyaev attacks naturalistic metaphysics and theology, for he finds Christian truth in the content of religious consciousness. This focuses on faith, belief and experience over reason. It implies the phenomenology of the conscious spiritual life. Hence, Berdyaev could say provocatively, "The experience of the saints gives to us a deeper understanding of human personality than the whole of metaphysics and theology put together."[1] As true as this may be, it does not imply that we are to minimize the importance of doctrine and religious philosophy. In fact, it may be that without them the saints would not have had a vital spiritual experience or something so relevant to their faith and life and so pertinent to their witness.

With these thoughts in mind we might well recall that Berdyaev does not affirm an abstract rationalistic ontology. Though he has a pattern of immanence it is not abstract, nor is it alien to divine transcendence. Unlike the abstract rationalistic scheme of Thomism, Berdyaev's immanentalism spells freedom of the spirit, not a rational scheme of form-in-matter but an ethical system of tensions and choices.

Before dismissing this topic may we ask: Is there anything more basic than freedom of the Spirit from which divine love and all divine virtues and attributes may be deduced? The Thomistic tradition has answered this affirmatively, for when looking to Aristotle it has asserted that the basic constituent of deity is Being—Being as a concept of human reason projected metaphysically. Does not this tradition confuse Being as rational form with God's Being or "isness"? Conceptually the being of God is identified with *Nous*, the rationally conceived substance of being and/or pure Form. Berdyaev would declare that the Thomistic idea of God as Being is a mere realistic objectification of an idea based on the perception of matter or material things, which are given form by the human mind so that on a high rung of the Aristotalics ladder of reality the concept is apotheosized by Thomists.

In addition, how could such an abstract ontology have place for the divine qualities of freedom, love, thought, will, intelligence and purpose? In short, how could such a product of reason have kinship with personality and the roles of the creator and redeemer? Furthermore, to say that God *is* does not demand that we identify as *isness* even God's own isness as the rational concept of Being objectively conceived and/or projected. Then, too, since God accounts for Being through beings by creation, then God is evil for having created things some of which are evil; evil then, is divine, for its reality or "isness" is of divine origin and consequence while related to other real things apart from which evil cannot be known. This places opposition between creation and Creator; also nature and Grace. On this basis there is no answer to the problem of good and evil. Once more the sufficiency of Thomism must be put in question. In general, it is unlikely that Thomism can reconcile *nous* with *pneuma* or reason and Spirit, or, for that matter, the world and Sophia. Its intention is respectable but not its metaphysical structure.

Though Barth and Berdyaev greatly differ in theology, both attack rationalism. Eric Mascall in *He Who Is* crystallizes them when he says that Barth finds rational theology to be anathama, because it assumes that finite, sinful man can comprehend a God who is incomprehensible, when grace and nature do not synthesise or merge. But to Berdyaev, rational theology is repudiated, because it "turns into an object of discussion a God who is already comprehended in the depths of the human spirit; whereby grace and nature are really identical." But the word "identical," here is a pro-monistic term, which is unfair to the two-in-one nature of God-manhood as held by Berdyaev and the existential two-in-one relation of time and eternity to which he subscribed. Berdyaev, after all, is neither a strict monist nor a harsh dualist. He is an ethical dualist of spirit; neither a rational ontology nor Manichean dualism does this justice.

Concerning the latter Berdyaev overtly states, "I do not recognize the dualism between spirit and matter for I do not believe in the autonomous reality of matter. The source of evil does not lie in matter as Plotinus thought, but in spirit itself."[2] Spirit and energy are more in accord than spirit and matter. Berdyaev's basic view of phenomenology can accept this. For him the highest reality is mental and spiritual, in short phenomenological, for it is of consciousness based on the primacy of subjectivity.[3]

Berdyaev not only saw cosmic evils objectively but viewed them subjectively by their consequences to men. They influenced human events and decisions as well as historical culture and social life as related to human response. Thus evils in nature were seen to affect the concrete existence of men. Yet the scientist sees death, for instance, as only a phenomenon of nature which terminates both nature and man. But as a man the scientist with his scientific views of death is still horrified by the thought of death because of his existential relation to it as a conscious person. This implies no real meaning to death or any cosmic evil from a scientific perspective. They are merely natural occurrences. Yet Berdyaev sees all cosmic evils as significant since related to man's life. Cosmic evils are never tragic save as they are significant to man i.e. not only natural but existentially pertinent. Man, then, has more than a cosmic view of evil. Even a scientific view of things is of little importance or even possibility apart from the existential perspective, i.e. its relevance to everyday life and the perspective of the conscious subject-self.

Communism neither provides nor seeks a victory over death. This is because it has no interest in personality. It is non-existential. It even kills the memory of the dead. Their funerals only glorify the state. With similar lack of respect for the person Communist morality only appertains to the social collective. Seeking to pose as scientific its pseudo-messianic Weltanschauung tries to control the human spirit and conscience by treating man as an object or machine.[4]

On the other hand, Christianity accepts the task of spiritualizing all social movements with a new spirit and outlook for social life. Regeneration of the person is extended in principle to all aspects of the social systems. Thus Christians must combat the social evils of the day including the meaninglessness of life promoted by Communism.[5] One of the major thrusts of Christians in this respect is the clarification of redemption and the overcoming of death, a major consequence of evil. To overcome evil is to take the sting out of death. Christ does this as he freely accepts death and defeats it. By this the transfiguration of life unto eternal life is made real.[6] Fear of death is overcome.

Phenomenology must be viewed as the primacy of consciousness deemed basic to all forms of knowledge. This emphasis sees man as a unique being, a knowing subject even in charge of objective or scientific empiricism. Consciousness gives priority to what it observes, yet what is observed is dependent epistemologically upon the observer, the conscious knower. Consciousness becomes basic, then, to the personal subject-self of existence as well as the interpretations of all things in philosophy. Apart from consciousness not much matters philosophically, scientifically or aesthetically. It is basic to the existence of the knower and cannot be avoided in any form of serious thought. It is the unique center of creative thought in whatever form, since consciousness is aware of phenomena of all sorts.

Notes

1. Berdyaev, *Freedom And The Spirit*, London, Geoffry Bles, 1935, p. 39.

2. Berdyaev, *Towards A New Epoch*, p. 11.

3. Berdyaev, *Freedom Amd The Spirit*, p. 6.

4. N. Berdiaeff, "Communist Secularism," *Christianity And The Crisis*, London, Victor Gallancz Ltd., 1933, pp. 583f, 565f, 579f.

5. *Ibid*, p. 584.

6. Berdyaev, *Freedom And The Spirit*, pp. 185–188.

Chapter VIII

Ethics and Meonic Freedom

One of Berdyaev's most unusual doctrines is his theory of "meonic freedom." It entails a pre-supposition of God in his creativeness. It is a type of opposition or cosmic friction as it were, with which God must reckon when asserting his creativeness. Berdyaev sees how it is also applied to moral problems and even the work of Christ. But religiously Berdyaev does not fully embrace an orthodoxy, for he is an original thinker who relates his views existentially to his experience and sensitivity to the tragic factors of life. He brings this forth in *The Destiny of Man* and *Freedom And The Spirit* (Chap. 5.) Fundamental is a basic irrational freedom, even implied in creation. Not merely "nothing," as some would view it, this is meonic freedom or pure possibility without determinism. So called "nothing" related to God and creation is a postulate implying what is fundamental to creation. It implies possibilities, even some resistance or cosmic friction, so to speak.

But this interpretation admittedly does not do justice to Berdyaev's intention to assert that God finds his creative act somewhat conditioned. Berdyaev regards creation as possible not only by the will of God but by the feat that an eternal potentiality of freedom accedes or consents to the act of creation. The term "meonic" is an Anglicized version of the Greek *to mé on* (from μη ὄν) or "not being," which not only implies a possibility of good creation but also evil and thus accounts for the evil which accompanies created existence. Creation is linked with freedom, but so is evil. As Edwin Lewis stated, "By creating through freedom (non-being or the principle of negation), God finds himself confronted with a situation which denies him-a situation in which freedom unrestrained appears as the evil which it is."[1] Lewis goes on to suggest that when God created man God created a rebel, and "God's creative act provides the opportunity for its own defeat." But God becomes a redeemer. Without freedom redemption would incur defeat. By his sacrificial love God transforms even meonic freedom, which both permits and hinders his purpose, and calls men to a similar love.[2]

Whatever else can be said of it, Berdyaev's dynamic theory of meonic freedom helps to protect the spiritual relationship between man and God. It is superior to the static category of Being held by the rationalists and retained in his way by Paul Tillich, who makes God appear as an "It." Meonic freedom may not be fully acceptable, but it is an attempt to preserve the dynamic character of the eternal Pneuma in a way not provided for by the Greek ontologies.

Berdyaev says, "Man is a free being and there is in him an element of primeval, uncreated, pre-meonic freedom. But he is powerless to his own irrational freedom and its abysmal darkness. This is his perennial tragedy.[3] The latter suggests what we referred to above as God's cosmic friction.

Berdyaev so much as says evil is due to "the unfathomable irrationality of freedom, in pure possibility."[4] So evil has no ontological origin, it is not objective but meonic. Berdyaev says, "This freedom is not a form of being which existed side by side with the Divine Being, the Logos or Mind. . . God created the world out of nothing, but it would be equally true to say that He created it out of freedom,"[5] i.e. meonic freedom. It is the latter that makes evil possible, it is non-being but distinguished from the original void. Evil is so pernicious, because it is so deceptive, always posing to be what it is not.

Berdyaev has a remarkable awareness of the fundamental problems of epistemology. "Thinkers," he says, "who devote themselves to epistemology seldom arrive at ontology."[6] Berdyaev himself is a thinker of this type and without regrets. He emphasizes that one can only start with being, not arrive at it. This is to start with life as it is known; it is to begin with human existence, not to arrive at reality but to begin with it.

In this existential approach to philosophy a critique of knowledge in any form is not something abstract but is one more vital creative experience, knowledge being a part of life.[7] This is to say that the object-subject relationship belongs to life, not to speculation alone. This, in turn, can be appreciated only in the light of Berdyaev's view of spirit and his spiritual conception of knowledge which implies that knowledge is an existential act, which both belongs to the knower and affects reality. "Reality is illumined through knowledge."[8] Being, which is subjective and spiritual, cognizes itself and is illumined from within.

Berdyaev agrees with Nicolas Hartmann that the subject as the knower belongs to fundamental reality; reality is not outside it. Being is not rationalized. It is not a categorized form of reason for Berdyaev, but as life it is prior to all rationalization; the starting-point of knowledge can not be the conclusion of a rational process. Rationalisms err in separating the knowing process from reality while equating concepts with objects. Knowledge itself for Berdyaev, is a part of reality, whereas in rationalism "knowledge is not something, but is about something." Berdyaev is profoundly existential here. He recognizes that only as knowledge is a part of being can even the knower be known. There have been some thinkers who have acknowledged this to some extent including Augustine, Pascal, Jacob Boehme and Kierkegaard, but the modern thinker who places himself above the process of knowledge and above what is known has a self that cannot be known.[9] We see the tendency to neglect this in the scientific laboratory. Behaviorism in psychology represents this, and any scientist or pseudo-scientist who denies mental subjectivity, makes purely objective observations but not without the use of logic and mathematics while at the same time forgetting that he cannot, on the basis of his assumptions, know himself, for he places himself beyond knowledge. This is the failure to see knowledge as an existential act. It is fundamental to the problem and perspective of the self, who may transcend parts of reality but not himself to which they belong or apart from which their knowledge and reality are irrelevant and unknowable-to-unreal. "Meaning is revealed to me," says Berdyaev, "only when I am in myself, i.e. in the spirit." On this basis external objectivity "does not exist for me." There can only be meaning in that which is in me and with me, i.e. in the spiritual world."[10] (to which the self belongs).

Philosophy, Berdyaev would say, cannot be oblivious to revelation. Though it is free, it is not autonomous in the sense of self-sufficiency. It must not be straightjacketed by preconceived rationalism but neither can it be blind to the fact that "Religious revelation means that being reveals itself to the knower."[11] Rather than the mere exercise of intellect to make moulds for the universe, philosophy must be based on spiritual insight and moral experience. To be true to its sources it must be as ethical and spiritual as it is logical. Whereas science assumes that to know being is apart from man the knower, true philosophy does not. "Therefore for philosophy being is spirit, and for science being is nature."[12]

Philosophical knowledge is not to be objectified, it is of the spiritual existential subject. Berdyaev does not refer to a subjectivity which is the complement of objectivity. The Ideas of Plato and Hegel, he explains, instead of being conceived as objective are rather to be seen as one's own concepts from within one's spirit-self. This is not to be confused with subjective idealism. "The conception of being which is not spirit, and is "without" and not "within," results in the tyranny of naturalism," Berdyaev asserts.[13] The world belongs to man, not man to the world. If not, how could the otherwise audacious idea of knowledge have occurred to him? This applies also to science. It does not imply subjective idealism, which confines man to the objectified world of nature. Meaning comes about through the creative activity of the knower. Any non-human ideal is meaningless, for meaning is of the creative spirit.

Berdyaev's view counters the German epistemologists, who make knowledge objectification by conceiving the knowing subject as the bearer of ideal unhuman forms and rational categories as if from outside of the subject's existence (like Kant and as the scientist assumes but fails to ask.) To objectify existence is to distort reality or rob it of meaning and to destroy true knowledge. Knowledge is rather a "communion" of being with being, for only being knows being. Neither Kant nor Hegel have answered the problem of how the validity of knowledge attributed by them to the superhuman realm of the transcendental unity of consciousness can be such. It is also something in the individual concrete man and related to the psychic element in man.[15] Hegel makes world-Reason, not only ultimate being but dissolves the knower by reducing man to a mere function of Reason. Berdyaev's idea of knowledge as spirit shows that such objectification is a destruction of both reality and man. There must be a kinship between the knower and the known, and this means reality is of the subject, not the object. For this to be true both reality and knowledge must be recognized as dynamically of spirit, belonging to an understanding and appreciation of the mystery of spiritual life and the entire universe. It is this to which neither monism nor ontological dualism can do justice.

Berdyaev's duality allows for the conception of a living God of Spirit rather than an abstract Absolute ideal. It means that only to the "symbolic and mythological consciousness," can the divine drama of existance be highly relevant.[16] This is what traditional rational theologies have failed to acknowledge or understand. Berdyaev maintains an ethical dualism and not an ontological dualism. It is a spiritual immanence. "Spirituality is the immanence of the Divine in the human, but this does not infer undifferentiated identity."[17] It includes supra-rationally the becoming of being and eternity in time. This temporal world has relative forms of the invisible world of the Spirit, the realm of the Being which Becomes. These are symbols or "copies" of true Being, not of a static Being as in Platonic thought but of true dynamic Being. Here is a paradoxical two-in-one dualism of the perfect order of the Spirit in contrast to the incomplete actualizations of the relative, finite and temporal orders. It is ultimate reality in relation to what is relative, yet real and creative as reality. It is the invisible within the visible. It includes the church mystical and triumphant in contrast to the Church historical and militant. It is good Spirit and a true subjectivity versus false objectification. Yet this is not an objective dualism rationally conceived but a subjective dualism mythologically portrayed. Contained within subjectivity it is decidedly existential.[18] It is expressed in symbols, because it recognizes the primacy of existence over essence. In addition, this unity-in-duality means a solution of the perennial problem of the one and the many so that the rational

question of the immanent versus the transcendent is to
Berdyaev on antiquated problem, for the one invades the other
in Berdyaev's dynamic eschatological and prophetic philosophy.[19] This is best seen from the standpoint of the relationship
of time and eternity, the understanding of which is fundamental to a justifiable appraisal of any cross-section of Berdyaev's
thought. A fair warning to the rationalist who seeks to criti-
cize Berdyaev would be this: Get off your rationalistic pedes-
tal if you wish to appraise honestly what is existential. Those
who dismiss Berdyaev as "vague," as one professor labeled him,
are unfair to his thinking and do not grasp the distinctiveness
of his existential thought. Even the Calvinist critic of Berdyaev
may be victimized by the harsh logic of his own position and
fail to use a clear-cut dialectics.

To express Berdyaev's unique two-in-one dualism from a
theological perspective, it is also well to see it in the light of
the meaning of love. Berdyaev speaks much of Eros and Agape.
Though he seldom uses the latter expression for the idea, his
view is very much in accord with Augustine's "Caritas," though
Berdyaev does not employ this term either. He sees a coordi-
nate relation between love as Eros and love as *philos* through
the highest type of love or *Agape*. This makes for the highest
motivation in applied ethics, for selfgiving and sacrifice provide it by qualifying the lesser loves. The combination of loves
amounts to an applied Caritas or activated charity. This is the
love St. Paul expressed in his "hymn of love" in I Corinthians
13. The basic spirit of Agápe makes these expressions of applied love essential to Christian ethics.

Parallels to this two-in-one love relationship are to be found
in the time and eternity relationship basic to time and
eschatology. The latter has been expounded in this author's
works, *Time And Its End*, and *Time, Existence and Destiny*, which
expose Berdyaev's most creative views in philosophy surrounding the philosophy of time.

It must be understood that Meonic freedom precedes being
i.e. it implies tenable alternatives or possibilities even before
creation. God even confronts it upon creating. This necessi-
tates the distinction between two freedoms. (1) irrational freedom which precedes good and evil making choice possible. As
meonic freedom this is uncreated and is an original mystery.

(2) rational freedom which is of God or universal Reason. It is a freedom in good being. The two freedoms correspond to the divine and the human.[20]

The first freedom is not a priori nor good nor evil. But it makes possible a reciprocal action between the divine and the human. Since Christ represents both natures in unity Christ can orient his followers towards God. Christ is the source of true freedom for man thru Grace and the Holy Spirit. Grace does not constrain us from without but illuminates us from within. Freedom and Grace collaborate. Grace enables human freedom to find perfect liberty in God thru Christ, the God-man.[21]

Freedom belongs to man's essence as spirit and is what most resembles God in man. Evil as suffering is the central problem of the religious conscience and is the obstacle in the existence of God. But Berdyaev says God exists only because of evil and suffering. The existence of evil is a proof of the existence of God. If the world consisted uniquely in the good and God were no more useful, the world itself would be God. God is because evil is. This is related to freedom. God is because freedom is.[22]

In the cross and resurrection Christ has given meaning even to suffering. The evil of death is vanquished and creation held captive. Christ both saves and continues creation as He orients man toward his creative vocation.[23] This is an eschatological and redemptive fulfillment especially aligned with *theosis*.

Notes

1. Edwin Lewis, *A Philosophy of the Christian Revelation*, Harper, N.Y., 1940, p. 280f.Cf. p. 125.

2. *Ibid*, p. 281.

3. Berdyaev, *The Destiny of Man*, p. 103.

4. Berdyaev, *Freedom And The Spirit*, p. 163.

5. Berdyaev, *Freedom And The Spirit*, p. 165.

6. Berdyaev, *Destiny of Man*, p. 1.

7. Berdyaev, *Destiny of Man*, p. 2.

8. Cf. Berdyaev, *Freedom And The Spirit*, p. 9.

9. Berdyaev, *Destiny of Man*, pp. 2, 3.

10. *Ibid*, p. 6.

11. Berdyaev, *Destiny of Man*, p. 4.

12. *Ibid*, p. 6.

13. *Ibid*, p. 7.

14. Berdyaev, *Destiny of Man*, p. 8.

15. *Ibid*, pp. 8-11.

16. Berdyaev, *Freedom And The Spirit*, chapter 6.

17. Berdyaev, *Spirit and Reality*, p. 133.

18. Berdyaev, Cf. *Towards A New Epoch*, p. 113.

19. Berdyaev, *The Divine and The Human*, p. 171 ff.

20. Eugene Porret, "Un Gnostique Moderne: Nicolas Berdiaeff," *Foi et Vie*, Paris, No. 2, 1938, (pp. 184-199), p. 191.

21. *Ibid*, pp. 192.

22. *Ibid*, p. 193.

23. *Ibid*, pp. 195-197.

Chapter IX

Ethics and Man's Fall

Man is composed of spirit, soul, mind and body. As a spirit he has an inner freedom,[1] which makes him more than a puppet of necessity. But his spirit is not a perceptible phenomenon, nor is it a higher form of the objective natural world. Spirit is more than an epiphenomenon of nature for Berdyaev, the way in which consciousness was claimed to be such among nineteenth century vitalists.[2] Spirit, rather, is freedom and is not even dependent upon social life for its basic existence. It is subject, not object. Spirit is freedom and is existentially the subject. No rational category, then, is applicable to spirit, human or divine. Since spirit is subject and not object, the philosophy of spirit cannot be an ontology but a philosophy of existence, of freedom rather than being or nature.[3] The spirit of man, then, should not be confused with either his psychic or corporeal nature, which are objective, for spirit is not a substance or objective entity so much as it is activity of the subject. It means that man is far more than a slave of cosmic forces of necessity and must be treated accordingly.

Spirit is not an ideal universal premise but is concretely personal and subjective. Spirit should be interpreted personalistically and existentially, not abstractly. It is not subject to universal laws of reason. It is prime reality and independent of thought.[4] Spirit allows for the spiritual, intuitive element in consciousness besides the psychological. Not only that but Berdyaev says Spirit is pneuma (breath or energy) which accounts for man's "inherent spiritual transcending principle,"[5] which makes his consciousness even more than the psyche and the ratio of his mind. Spirit is divinely infused. *Pneuma* is to the soul what blood is to the body. Spirit is the prime reality of freedom and creativeness; it is qualitative, not quantitative.

Berdyaev's thought has much in common here with Dostoevsky. Perhaps through Dostoevsky more than any other thinker Berdyaev came to see man as far more than a natural phenomenon superior to other phenomena. Like Dostoevsky he conceives man to be a microcosmos, the center of being, which is spirit, and in whom centers the riddle of all existence. To solve the problem of man is to solve the problem of God, while on the other hand, if there is no God there is no man. This strange antinomy can be resolved only as human destiny is referred to Christ, the God-man. Such an anthropological view, Berdyaev maintains, was not possible in the ancient world of pagan philosophy and religion but only in the Christian world.[7] Man as microcosmos blends with the existential character of the thinking of both Dostoevsky and Berdyaev. Both subscribe to a dynamic anthropology, which asserts that life is understood only by those who are involved in its maelstrom and do not ignore it by projecting themselves in their ideas beyond it. Here is where the problem of epistemology is so important to the problem of human freedom in relation to all established ethical standards and metaphysical objectifications in life and thought. Berdyaev then strongly asserts that ". . . society is an infinitesimal part of personality, its social element: the whole world forms part of a person. It is not society and nature but the person, who is the existential centre."[8] Thus, man is a microcosm of the macrocosm.

Berdyaev maintains that the Orthodox church is the most like primitive Christianity, for it is the least secularized. It is not confined to an authoritative structure like the Catholic Church. It has a spiritual tradition that is inward rather than outward. The individual is within the organismic Body of Christ and in union with others. Protestants are apt to question this view to some extent, because Orthodox sacerdotalism is so structural.

The real heretic is not necessarily the one who espouses false doctrine but the one whose spiritual life is askew. Orthodoxy, says Berdyaev, is much less legalistic than other denominations and is more experientially mystical than intellectual. It aims at transfiguration through the immanental presence and action of the Holy Spirit in creation, yet it sharply separates the divine from the world of nature or the Kingdom of God from the kingdom of Caesar. Though man and nature are not God, neither are they removed from God.[9]

Orthodoxy is freedom of spirit and conscience and is not legalistic. Yet it is not individualistic but unified by Grace. Thus it is akin to a cosmic transfiguration. The resurrection is more basic even than the crucifixion, hence Easter is more important than Christmas. Transfiguration is held to be more important than justification. It is more closely related to eschatological fulfillment in the Kingdom, which not only is but is to come. Berdyaev thinks orthodoxy is most favorable to the ecumenical union of the churches of the East and West.[10]

Yet Berdyaev was unusually sensitive to the tendency of leaders to link ecumenicity at times with nationalism and internationalism. This is sometimes related to Christian universalism. The philosophical danger here is an idolatry, which proclaims a relative idea to be an absolute. This is akin to the failure to keep alive the distinction between the natural man and the spiritual man. This obsession is linked with a demented naturalistic view, which overlooks the kinship between God and the inner man. Nationalism feeds on this contradiction, but true ecumenicity does not.[11] Quite early in his career Berdyaev wrote, "Truth and justice are absolute and are rooted in the transcendent; they are not of social origin."[12] In his early period Berdyaev was one who sought the Absolute. When he became a Christian he found it, after inward struggles and some doubts. Finding the Absolute by faith helped him to embrace the ideals mentioned but not as coldly rational principles but as expressions of divine truths related to existence and faith.[13] This really was an aspect of his existential perspective-in-the-making.

Berdyaev's down-to-earth perspective was related to his appreciation for Henrik Ibsen's "feeling for life." Together Ibsen and Dostoevsky aroused in Berdyaev a sensitivity to the inner aspects of the self to which religion often made appeals. This, in turn offset rationalistic views and made these writers ones who helped thinkers to re-consider Christ and Orthodoxy.

Looking to the Church Berdyaev took on concern for Sobornost (togetherness), a creative type of brotherhood and catholicity which promoted more freedom in the church together with concern for social transfiguration and eschatological possibilities. All the while Berdyaev was anthropological more than metaphysical and cosmological. He also came to see the dialectical issues in the Christian revelation, which conceded the roles of paradox over rationalism.

Being a social ethicist Berdyaev could appreciate the intensification of spiritual thought in Russia, but he also saw how religious leaders often lacked empirical concern for the transformation of society. On the other hand, Berdyaev saw how many Christian leaders failed to see the positive side of the Marxist revolution. Berdyaev was one among few who could say, "The problem of bread is not only a material, but a spiritual one."[14] Yet he himself did not seek an abstract system of thought for categorizing all things but had a personal existential view of specific problems with which to address the Christian conscience. Inner questionings were to Berdyaev more important than abstract speculations. These were seen involved in the struggles and sufferings of everyday existence. Bourgeois smugness and lackadaisicalness were often an attitude of self-satisfaction that spelled the lack of ethical courage.[15]

Berdyaev applauded all persons who assumed responsibilities toward their fellow men. Often this demanded a recognition of the tragic side of life. But evolutionary progress was not deemed the solution so much as were personal and social commitments to "the transcendent ultimates" or revealed absolutes. These enhanced ethical concerns and activated responsibility for them.

While positivism was mounting in the West, it was almost stifled in Russia. The main reason was that Russian thinkers were turning to Christ early in the 20th century as related to their existential perspectives. Khomiakov had a broader version of Orthodoxy which many found innovative and reforming. Meanwhile Berdyaev's thought became anchored to God-manhood as the starting point in religious philosophy and theology.[16] Though God is related to man in the incarnate Christ, God is ever transcendent. God-manhood is a mystery with a paradoxical coincidence of opposites correlating and uniting what reason cannot, viz the two-in-one relation of God and man.[17] Metaphysical theory could not do justice to this mystery of transcendence within immanence. Serviceable to it is the existential perspective which breaks with abstractions and reckons with the immediate concerns of life.

Though he was humanistically interested in the search for truth in man, Berdyaev's pivotal point was always Christ, the God-man. He saw that the discovery of reality is a matter of spiritual discernment. Spiritual realities are not revealed to us like objects, for cognition itself is "a creative act of the spirit."[18] This relates to what transcends man as well as to his inner self-transcendence. It is an inward process, not of outward or extraneous phenomena, which psychologically reduce man to aspects of the objectified or material world. Berdyaev's pneumatology viewed man as a free spirit while related to God and other men accordingly. He stated in his work, *Freedom And The Spirit*, that man's spirit is not a finalized substance but is existence transcending subjectively all finite categories. Thus, one can only begin inwardly with God and not claim to find God at the end of a string of syllogisms or arguments. Berdyaev, then, identifies philosophy with mysticism including gnosis or intuitive insight into the meaning of things. To Berdyaev mysticism is knowledge based on "immediate contact with the ultimate reality." This, in turn, implies that man has an interaction with God. The divine and the human orders respectively are not fixed with finality, so man can be changed as well as he can change creatively the conditions of life. Berdyaev views this mythologically, whereby a reciprocal relation exists between man and God centered around God-manhood and/or the incarnate Christ.

It is by virtue of man's freedom that he can rise to new heights or fall to lower ones. Even Berdyaev's metaphysics, as he once said to Evgueny Lampert of Oxford, is a design to help guarantee man's freedom.

The Fall of man is to Berdyaev a moment in the growth of consciousness; not only a moral lapse or sin on the part of Adam, it is an obsession with the natural man's state of egocentricism. Man fell away from paradise as a state of unconscious harmony with the cosmos, while, for the sake of gaining a fuller life, he preferred the trial and error of life linked with knowledge to the pseudo-blissful life of ignorance. Consciousness, which is basic to personality, implies various types of pain, but through it man can reach the fullness of life. Conflicts between individual life and the generic cosmic forces imply the struggle between consciousness and sub-consciousness central to human personality including sex life and social tensions. It is tension not only between good and evil but different kinds of good. For Berdyaev this implies not only freedom but paradoxical issues which must not be obviated in concrete existence. Natalie Duddington says, "Berdyaev brings out better perhaps than any other modern writer that the Christian ideal is not a dutiful observance of divinely prescribed rules of conduct, but a free and spontaneous expression which is the image and likeness of God."[19] Legalism in religion is repudiated in favor of ethical freedom and personal faith as commitment.

Berdyaev has seen where the myth of the fall of man is very expressive. Not a literalistic truth, it is a truth conveyed in story form. It suggests how God was unable to avert the evil resulting from a freedom which he did not create, the meonic freedom, which was presupposed by God in his very act of creation. Berdyaev sees, as already inferred, that it was a type of "friction," since it implied a kind of competitiveness in the matter of evil's possibility.

Berdyaev regarded the fall of man as having preceded and not having followed the production of the natural world. It was an event which occasioned tensions through "the dividedness, multiplicity and externality of the world" as suggested by Pythian-Adams. It was an event in the spiritual world causing what he calls the "bad infinity of time."[20] Though not to be literalized as in an orthodox view the fall leading to a type of inherited corruption or proclivity to sin it is at least symbolic of the existential fallenness of man in which his egoism and selfishness become conditions of bias and bigotry. These conditions affect both the person and his world.

"Man preferred death and the bitterness of discrimination to the blissful and innocent life of ignorance. . ." said Berdyaev. Also "the paradox of Christian consciousness is that Christ would not have appeared in the life of paradise. . . . If man had remained in the passive state of paradisiacal innocence and unconsciousness . . . he would not have known Christ or attained deification."[21] The latter refers to theosis or the return to unity with God.

Berdyaev boldly claims that "the pre-cosmic fall of man was the occasion of the creation of this world order." He declares, "The fall could not have taken place in the natural world, because this world is itself the result of the Fall."[22] It took place in the spiritual meonic world before time began. It produced time as we think of it.

Berdyaev is not so inclined to expound a theology as an anthropology. Man and his sufferings are basic to the theme of the God-man. "Christianity is the religion of the divine Trinity and God-humanity. It presupposes faith in man as well as in God. . . . It exalts man . . . at the center of being (and the) organizations of the world."[23] When humanism appeared it fostored a tragedy by exalting man to the point of self-sufficiency and separating him from his true center in God. This provided the seeds of human destruction spiritually and culturally. The blame for this tragedy cannot and need not be pin-pointed. It began with the self-consciousness of man in medieval thought and its sanctification of the natural. This was a search for theocracy, but it failed,[24] being under law, not Grace.

The Fall of man is a mythological expression of a basic problem in human existence. As such it is a story that is believed to express a serious truth. The myth of the Fall implies not only a problem for man but a problem for God. This implies God's inability to avert the evil resulting from the meonic freedom, which God did not create but confronted when he created all things including man. Berdyaev has recognized that the Fall preceded, rather than followed, the creation of the natural world. The divisions and multiplicities of the world are the result of the Fall, which took place not in our natural world but in the spiritual world and plunged it into a state of temporal evils.[25]

As Berdyaev observes, there is always a desire to humiliate man in traditional theology by abusing the idea of the Fall. Actually, as Berdyaev states, "The idea of the Fall is at bottom a proud idea."[26] The responsibility for evil exalts man instead of humiliating him. It implies that he has a tremendous power of freedom capable of even rising against God, of separating itself from him, of "creating hell and a godless world of its own."[27] In addition man's rejection of Eden contributed to the birth of consciousness.

It must be realized that Berdyaev was not as interested in clarifying theology as anthropology. Man is the one he defends and even exalts. Man has an innate freedom and creativity contributing to his destiny. Yet man is himself fallen while a combination of the divine and human. He is at the center of being and the organized world, "The world is itself the result of the Fall," says Berdyaev.[28] Though fallen the world is not altogether corrupt. Nor is man.

Notes

1. Cf. Slaatte, *Modern Science and The Human Condition*, pp. 109ff, 118f.

2. Berdyaev, *Spirit and Reality*, pp. 1ff, 177.

3. *Ibid*, p. 4f, 14.

4. *Ibid*, p. 12, 14, 31, 189.

5. *Ibid*, p. 15, 28.

6. *Ibid*, p. 21.

7. *Dostoevsky*, p. 39, 45, by Berdyaev.

8. Nicolas Berdyaev, *Communism and Christians*, p. 202.

9. N. Berdiaff, "The Truth of Orthodoxy," *The Student World*, July, 1928, pp. 249-263, esp. pp. 249-250.

10. *Ibid*, p. 253-259.

11. N. Berdiaeff, "Christianity, Nationalism and The State," *World's Youth*, Vol. X, No. 3, Oct. 1934. YMCA Geneva, Switzerland, pp. 223-226.

12. Cited by Donald Attwater, editor, "Modern Christian Revolutionaries," by Evgueny Lampert, p. 314.

13. *Ibid*, p. 321.

14. *Ibid*, p. 321.

15. Berdyaev, *Spirit and Reality*, p. 6f.

16. Berdyaev, *Freedom And The Spirit*, Chap. 6.

17. *Ibid*, Chaps. 5 and 6.

18. Berdyaev, *Spirit and Reality*, p. 7f.

19. Duddington, "Philosophy in Russia," *Philosophy*, Vol. VII, 1932, pp. 218ff; 250.

20. Berdyaev, *Freedom And The Spirit*, pp. 101-103, 91, 135; Berdyaev, *The Destiny of Man*, p. 34.

21. Berdyaev, *The Destiny of Man*, p. 46f, Cf. p. 35–38.

22. Berdyaev, *Freedom and the Spirit*, p. 22.

23. *Ibid*, p. 206.

24. *Ibid*, p. 206, 230f.

25. *Ibid*, pp. 221ff, p.313. Cf. pp. 216 f. Cf. Berdyaev, *The End of Our Time*, p. 15f.

26. Berdyaev, *Freedom And The Spirit*, pp. 161–163, 169, Cf. pp. 17–21, 132.

27. Berdyaev, *The Destiny of Man*, p. 35.

28. Ibid, p.48f; *Freedom And The Spirit*, pp. 22, 206.

Chapter X

Ethics and Social Evils

One of the most serious of social evils of modern times is that of race prejudice. Yet racism has neither scientific grounds nor sound philosophical basis. In Germany it included anti-Semitism, an old disease of the German temperament. Berdyaev states that it gave witness to the fact that Christianity never really succeeded in changing the depths of German paganism.

The philosopher Johann Fichte held German culture to be the highest type, yet he was anti-Semitic. Hegel was strongly in favor of the purely German mission to the world. Hitler became a strong anti-Semitic leader and was inspired by the German messianism of Wagner's music akin to Nietzsche's super-race theory of Übermensch.[1]

But science sees the race theory to be false. There is no pure race as such, though the Hebrews have come closest to it. A true Christian cannot rightly be a racist.[2] There is need of a new spirituality to heal this tension. Intellectuals feel nearly helpless with too little material support for eradicating this problem. The elite are left to adapt themselves to the lower tastes of the masses. In order to have a moral and social elevation toward blending the aristocratic and democratic levels of life the religious renaissance must promote a cultural renaissance.[3] Implied here is a necessary judgment on both humanity and Christianity toward a transfiguration of society.

Sadism and masochism are often reflected in the same egocentric manner. However, bread for myself is a material quest;

bread for expressions of love is a spiritual quest, as Berdyaev reminds us.[4] As for expressions of love, often Christians have debased the meaning of love as related to sex and marriage, though they have been lenient about property rights. Thus the study of Christian anthropology is much-needed today. It is basic to the preservation of human dignity. A purer Christianity is needed to enhance this. It calls for the new freedom of Spirit through the new spirituality which fostors social transfiguration in keeping with the fulfillment of the Kingdom.

Berdyaev rightly saw the need for recovered respect for personality. He saw that today there is need for combining respect for the person with concern for the community to overcome all forms of depersonalization. Only a Christian Renaissance of this type could overcome "the dehumanization which threatens the world."[5] This demands a more than naturalistic view of man. It also implies a combined social ethics and spiritual revival to promote cultural responsibilities. Berdyaev believed that the historic aims and destiny of the Russian people favored a social order more just than that of the West. He saw how the sacred elements of life must be asserted from within the secular to leaven it with the spirit of Christ. The Church must send out committed and disciplined people aglow with the Holy Spirit and the inspiration to clean up the evils of society. No longer should religion be regarded as solely each person's private affair; it must be concerned about all people and help them meet their material, social and moral needs.

Berdyaev supports the view of Leon Bloy who said to Christians, in view of the Hitlerian atrocities, "We forget, or rather we do not wish to know, that our God-made man is a Jew . . . that the Apostles were Jews, as well as all the Prophets; and finally that our whole sacred Liturgy is drawn from Jewish books. In consequence, how may one express the enormity of the outrage and blasphemy of vilifying the Jewish race."[6]

As a prophetic and messianic religion Christianity's human origins spring from the Jewish people. The Aryans were neither messianic nor prophetic. In time German anti-Semitism evolved into an anti-Christian movement. Yet the Jews must be applauded for their survival as a people. A materialistic explanation is impossible. Christians have been much at fault and should help defend the Jews while challenged by the Christian Gospel and its ethics. All nationalisms should be condemned by it, for the Gospel is favorable to universalism.[7]

It is true, however, that Jews backed the crucifixion of Christ, since the incarnation of God was deemed by them to be false. Yet social justice was propounded by Judaism. The contemporary Jewish objection against Christianity is that its message cannot be fulfilled; its morals are so high that they conflict with human nature. Jews also point legitimately to the inconsistencies in the social life of Christians as being so unlike the teachings of Christ.[8]

Another ethical issue which concerns Berdyaev is the violence frequently occurring in modern societies. He repudiates violence yet endorses certain kinds of social pressure and propaganda toward the reformation of society. He frankly desires to see both capitalism and communism superceded through a new and different kind of political institution, which will combine the virtues of democratic and aristocratic governments. This implies a simpler material culture blended with a more complex spiritual type.

Included in this position, Berdyaev desires a new form of asceticism which will temper capitalism. He does not favor the abolition of private property but is against its socio-economic control by large private fortunes and businesses. Competition, he believes, should be replaced by cooperation or cooperative movements like some of the better aspects of the American economic system. Berdyaev predicts that, as such improvements are made, the old type of craft-guilds will re-appear, and town and country will be linked more strongly. Groups based on trades and arts will replace the present castes and classes. Social systems like monarchy, aristocracy and democracy (as presently known) will end and be replaced by a natural "hierarchism" based on innate differences in human capacities. Berdyaev states that the social groupings just referred to will end. Distinctions based on birth and wealth will be wiped out. A spiritual aristocracy will be more qualitative, and social power will be put in the hands of the people.

Above all, religion will not be based on an ecclesiastical hierarchy but a faith-conditional spiritual communion inspiring all human activity. Not a rationally devised earthly paradise, since Berdyaev is too much of a realist, who sees all mundane affairs influenced spiritually while not overnight by any kind of fiat,[9] but a growth in spiritual freedom and prophetic faith. An earnest qualitative minority must needs lead the way to influence the quantitative majority. Spiritual freedom as opposed to any kind of compulsion will be stressed. Legalisms will be replaced by the ethics of creativeness based upon a combination of grace and freedom as the Holy Spirit is introduced into every sphere of life.[10]

Also related to violence and classisms is the dreaded occurrences of war. It is an irrational activity, thinks Berdyaev, and cannot be eradicated apart from what Leo Tolstoy's emphasis upon non-resistance prompted by religious faith. Berdyaev respected the stance taken by Tolstoy yet finds it impossible to maintain that in all circumstances it will succeed. Needed today, Berdyaev says, is an "active resistance to war."[11]

There are two sides of the problem. (1) War must be condemned by the Christian conscience as the greatest of all evils. (2) War must be stopped in a practical way, this being the more difficult aspect. Berdyaev states, "It is hard to believe that it would be possible to abolish war and the will-to-war in our capitalist order of society, with these nationalistic states which all affirm their sovereignty."[12] The social order must be changed to make war obsolete. Marxists are not all wrong here, but they fail to take seriously the idea that we must begin with the thinking of the individual, for it is the case that the underlying struggle is in the souls of men, while the battle continues on social levels. Berdyaev saw how the League of Nations failed to consider the spiritual question.[13] (Perhaps the post-World War II perspective is more hopeful, since the United Nations charter was strongly initiated and written up by the Christian philosophy of young people in the Youth Fellowship of the Methodist Church.) Berdyaev overtly asserts that the freer denominations take stands against war more readily than do the heads of churches allied with states. He points out that Augustine, Calvin and Luther justified war on such grounds as these: Old Testament precedents; good citizenship, and citizens being subjects of the state. A good sign today is the refusal of some Christians to participate in warfare. All "romanticism about war" must be eradicated such as the colorful youth movements of Fascism.[14]

From the Christian perspective neighbors are no less than prospective brothers in Christ. This is different from the humanistic attitude of social determinism, since the individual person matters to the Christian. The conscientious objectors are not like sheep but creative heroes since not passive in the face of war.[15] The struggle against war is a spiritual one. It relates to what people are committed to in their hearts.

One of the more subtle evils of society is what has been called "the social lie." This is a type of myth causing people to lie either consciously or unconsciously. It is prompted, says Berdyaev, by forms of fear, while often as a "protective weapon."[16]

Most significant is the social lie which is commonly viewed as duty. The masses hold some myths in their consciousness. Early myths were deliberate falsehoods accepted almost unconsciously, and organized society often has falsehood at its base. Nietzsche maintained that truth is born of the will to power; Marx said it is born of the economic struggle. Pragmatists say that it is a product of what is deemed useful. The criteria of truth in any case is the increase of power. To acquire power falsehood may prove more useful than truth at times. Even technology is a search for power.[17]

Tolstoy's writings are directed against the social falsehoods integrated with civilization. Freud created the myth of the Oedipus Complex involved in the explanation of the origins of society. Apart from his contributions to science Freud's philosophy cannot justify his own love of truth, which is against false ideas. Berdyaev states, "Science tends to deny religious realities as myths born of the collective sub-conscious. But science itself has created the myth of universal knowledge capable of solving all problems." Science loves the truth, but "scientism" is false.[18]

The strong role of falsehood in our time is part of the change in our consciousness, viz the "exteriorization of conscience." Berdyaev states, "When conscience, the organ (capacity) of moral judgment, is transferred from the depths of individual personality, to the collective . . . then any falsehood may seem justified." In the past falsehood has been used by the collective conscience of the state, the church or the class, the party or the military, but never like today. Personal conscience is paralyzed especially by the state, hence, its character is changing. People are under constraints to support "the collective good." Most falsehood of this type is related to the central collectives in search of power.[19]

The worst aspect of this trend is that by falsehood society determines the spirit of people. Diplomacy is not the key to a new more honorable society, for today society confronts us with too many lies and fabrications. Needed is the spiritual inspiration of conscience to fell the wild notions that feed on falsehoods. Nietzsche accentuated the mendaciousness of society. Kierkegaard acknowledged its presence but refused to settle for it; Berdyaev likewise. They saw the need and possibility of a Christian conscience to offset such socially applied fabrications.

Notes

1. Berdyaev, *The Meaning of History*, p. 85f.

2. *Ibid*, pp. 97, 101.

3. *Ibid*, pp. 111, 109–130.

4. *Ibid*, pp. 121–123.

5. *Ibid*, p. 113f.

6. Berdyaev, "Christianity and Anti-Semitism," *Blackfriars*, Oxford, October 1948, p. 451ff.

7. *Ibid*, p. 452ff.

8. *Ibid*, pp. 455, 459, 461–465.

9. Berdyaev, *Christianity And Class War* (and) *The End of Our Time*, pp. 105f, 116, 119.

10. Berdyaev, *Spirit And Reality*, Pt. II.

11. Berdyaev, "War And The Christian Conscience," essay in pamphlet form in series *Pay Pamphlets*, No. 2, James Clarke and Co., Ltd., London, 1938.

12. *Ibid*, p. 2.

13. *Ibid*, p. 3.

14. *Ibid*, pp. 5, 6, 7.

15. *Ibid*, pp. 10–12f.

16. Berdyaev, "The Paradox of Falsehood," *Christendom*, Vol. IV, Autumn, 1939, no. 4, p. 494ff.

17. *Ibid*, pp. 495–497.

18. *Ibid*, pp. 497–499.

19. *Ibid*, pp. 499–500.

PART THREE

ETHICS AND
PHILOSOPHICAL ISSUES

Chapter XI

Subjectivity and Objectification

Expressed in his book *Spirit And Reality* Nicholas Berdyaev was sensitive to the "spiritual distress" basic to the contemporary crisis in mainly Western society. He was much concerned about a remedy and saw a spiritual awakening to be essential thereto, for he believed it is the only way of overcoming "our ultimate spiritual death" based on our enslavement to materialistic ideas and mechanisms often regarded as objectification.

Associated with this cultural nemesis is the tendency of academic people to naively regard spirit as only an epiphenomenon of something naturalistic. But spiritual phenomena are not reducible to objective reality the way rational philosophies are prone to treat them by objectifications. Yet this is not to deny a spiritualistic ontology, which views spirit as being; it merely disassociates itself from concepts which are conceived objectively like nature. "In the Kantian system there are, however, the latent possibilities of an existential philosophy emancipated from any kind of naturalistic metaphysics," said Berdyaev. "Kant himself did not exploit these possibilities to the full."[1] Existentially, reality is not valued by emphasizing the object but the action of the subject. Spirit is neither an object nor rational category of being. "The philosophy of spirit," says Berdyaev, "should not be a philosophy of being or an ontology, but a philosophy of existence." Existence involves particulars and moral choices of the knowing self or subject. Spirit is freedom rather than nature. Since it is not objective reality, it is easy for some to deny it, for they remain partial to objectivity. God is spirit, for He is not object but subject, which is primary existence and is purposive. The basic reality of spirit is existential, not realistic or idealistic.[2]

Usually, the realist forgets that the subject participates in being and, says Berdyaev, is himself existentially involved in the knowledge of reality. As such the subject includes not only reason in knowledge but also the will. Existentially, reality is not a creation of knowledge, but knowledge is a creative art, so objective reality depends upon the knowing subject and his existential character. Spirit is revealed through the existential subject. Realism fails to consider the contributions of the knowing subject. It objectifies things too much, whereas spirit is personal and subjective; it is personalistic and comes to life in personality freed from determinisms since not governed by universal laws of reason. The human mind is not an abstract *ratio* but is spirit, for consciousness is not merely a psychological concept but is fundamentally a spiritual element, which includes a super-consciousness within consciousness.[3]

Berdyaev regards spirit as pneuma, not nous. Not merely human consciousness or thought, it is a state inspired by divine inspiration. As in the New Testament it is identifiable with the Holy Spirit who discloses the Kingdom of God. Spirit is dynamic power basic to authentic religious faith and life. It is a divine element infused into man. Early Christian theologians, influenced by the Greeks, misinterpreted the soul as *nous*, and not until Augustine was it conceived as *pneuma* or spiritual substance. Later in the 19th century Hegel's position made pneuma a spiritualized objectification or "philosophical spiritualization." Spirit as freedom and creativeness was stultified by this.

Yet post-Kantian German philosophy saw freedom as the main attribute of spirit. Hegel associated it with reason as identified with God. But as a universalist Hegel failed to apprehend the mystery of personality and its relation to spirit as one spirit to another. His philosophy, therefore, failed to express the personal relationship of man with God. Berdyaev states, "An ontologically orientated Weltanschauung is static, whereas a pneumatologically orientated one is dynamic. Existential philosophy is not an ontological philosophy in the traditional sense of the word."[4] It is more like a communication between spirits or persons.

Hence, Berdyaev was sensitive to the difference between the God of Abraham, Isaac and Jacob, on the one hand, and the God of the philosophers like Spinoza and Hegel, on the other. Basic is the search for the individual person who is free rather than necessitated and universalized by laws of reason. Personality is superior to nature and the object or thing, for it is spirit, not nous but pneuma. Hence, too, the Christian doctrine of resurrection is not of the physical body but a "new spiritual body," as St. Paul speaks of it. More than immortality it is a personalistic life of spirit for the whole man and not abstractly for the soul alone.[5]

Berdyaev sees concrete human existence as more basic than rationally perceived being. This is because man is the reasoner within existence. His knowledge is existentially human. Popular enslavement to rational and materialistic knowledge is inferior. Consciousness is basic to what is human and existential, hence true philosophy is consciously anthropocentric, while man, the thinker, is theocentric, for he transcends and is transcended. Consciousness is thereby made possible as the seat of knowledge, creativity and morality. Being not only conforms to reason's laws, as the Greeks insisted, but is integral to concrete everyday existence. Truth is related to the orientation of consciousness. Philosophy, therefore, cannot evade the knowing self. We cannot have a neutral philosophy removed from consciousness. Hence, even religion influences philosophy. The neutrality of reason as in rationalism is a fiction. Philosophy is a struggle in favor of values overtly known. Especially the humanities are less objective and call for more fellowship among knowers. Where greater fellowship prevails higher spiritual truths are found. Abstract ideas are isolated from existence. Truth is knowledge that includes the spiritualization of emotions and will. This is akin to both the Eastern Fathers and Pascal's emphasis upon "the heart." Knowledge cannot be kept remote from the heart.[6] The heart's reasons can modify reason itself. Not of an isolated world man is a microcosm, and in his existence as subject is reflected the mystery of the world. So, basic to philosophy is the philosopher himself as existentially conditioned. Hence existential philosophy can illuminate all objectifications from within. By this all metaphysical naturalism is negated. Truth is found in the subject, not the object. "Being can only be revealed in existence." Even objective knowledge is really subjective as a product of the knowing self created by God. Pascal in his *Pensees* said, "The heart has reasons that reason does not know." Thus the existential perspective of knowledge precedes the rationalist view; it is basic to all knowledge.

Objectification is a depersonal projection of what is temporal into something ideal. It makes for a world fabricated out of rational concepts and what is standardized for society. It applies less to physical levels of life. Opposed to such thought is creative thought and spiritual life. Objectification is the death of authentic knowledge or inward illumination produced in being. This is because man is not merely a piece of the objective world, for he exists subjectively beyond the objective realm. Hence opposed to objectifications is man becoming creative.[7] Berdyaev sees a more existential view of knowledge related to the whole self. Here he is aligned with Kierkegaard in stressing the preeminence of subjectivity. Religious existentialism centers in this. Abstraction is replaced by concrete moral and spiritual experience. It is life and not system. It is not academic so much as intuitive and creative experience. "The creative act is not only a struggle against sin and evil but is the creation of a new world by a free act."[8] "Spirit breaks the chains of necessity in this world."[9]

Objective knowledge is necessitative, and it reduces man to but a part of nature, a thing or something impersonal. It isolates a person and makes him no longer a self among other selves, who have communion with selves. It reduces the self to an *it* or the impersonal *das Man* of Heidegger's thought. Objectivity prevents thought from being a free and creative activity.

Berdyaev puts volition above intellect, for it often controls reason. Knowledge is Eros plus Logos. This disallows the dominance of truth as objective. A vital communion of 'I' and 'Thou' is basic. Berdyaev could see that a rational knowledge of the spiritual is impossible, yet the spiritual as suprarational should not be alienated from the problem of knowledge. Knowledge is far more than the relation of thought to being. Being must be conceived as interior, not exterior. It is of the spirit emanating from the existential knowing subject.

Whenever the subject objectifies a concept, often under the influence of the emotions, it forms an illusary object, which belongs to the process of objectification, which spells epistemological disintegration. This is a fallen state, a pseudo-projection of the object, a process which realism has overlooked. It remains blind to the involvement of the subject in this process and falsely externalizes reality.[10] Objectification is inadequate, for it submerges the primacy of the knowing and creative subject. Very little matters or has significance apart from the subject, though realism overlooks this. Nothing can displace the basic creativity of the subject, whose world this is while preeminently in the Spirit. Until this is freely acknowledged everywhere our culture will continue to weaken ethically. Personal subjectivity must be kept primary in all relationships, lest our culture dry up and die on the vine of creative endeavors overshadowed by objectivity.

Objectification especially weakens the life of the spirit. Reliance upon material things effected by the Fall of the world leads to this. Roman Catholic sacramentalism caters to this weakness, Berdyaev contends. Contrary to Catholic transsubstantiation, material things are not channels of Grace, though they can be associated. Metaphorically, electricity and the appliances which convey it are not identical, though related or even interrelated. This two-in-one interrelationship does not make for an identification or synthesis of the factors involved but a close-knit association. Not an objective synthesis or unity, this is primarily a subjective association or paradox which makes for a faith-conditioned blessing.

Notes

1. Berdyaev, *Spirit and Reality*, p. 4.

2. *Ibid*, p. 5.

3. *Ibid*, pp. 6-14.

4. *Ibid*, pp. 15, 21, 25.

5. Berdyaev, *Preface*, Adolphe Lazareff, *Vie et Connaissance*, p. 5-7; also Berdyaev, "Marxism And The Conception of Personality," *Christendom*, Oxford, Vol. V, No. 21, March, 1936, pp. 35-40.

6. Berdyaev, *Spirit And Reality*, pp. 206, 223, 215, 211-213, 236. Also Berdyaev, *The Divine And The Human*, pp. 10, 53, 44, 192; and Berdyaev, *Solitude And Society*, p. 47f.

7. Berdyaev, *Freedom And The Spirit*, p. 15, 32, 139. Berdyaev, *Slavery And Freedom*, pp. 8, 11, 15. Berdyaev, *Destiny Of Man*, p. 11.

8. Berdyaev, *Der Sinn des Schaffens*, p. 99.

9. *Ibid*.

10. Berdyaev, *Spirit And Reality*, pp. 8-10, 31.

Chapter XII

Subjectivity and Philosophy

Philosophically, both the bourgeois outlook and the view of the proletariat have been prone to minimize the meaning and importance of personality by subjugating it to social, economic and governmental forces and studies. Commonly, personality has been objectified and dehumanized not only by scientific psychology but historic social processes which subordinate man to the state, race, class or nation. These are "fatal for personality," as Berdyaev puts it.[1] Also, technologies and capitalism are here involved as they tend to promote what men live for materialistically.

"Loss of faith in God has led to a loss of faith in man" states Berdyaev.[2] One mark of this is a decreasing sensitivity to sin, much of which is social in nature. Some thinkers like Heidegger and Freud stress the decadence involved in evils but not as sin, since they place society above God and persons.[3] Dehumanization also occurs in Karl Barth's neo-orthodox theology, since for him the *imago dei* is destroyed. Berdyaev sees, too, how the state of the intelligentsia suffers morally by placing money first. A cultural renaissance can come about only through "the resurrection of spiritual forces," he says, for in our time "the human being has ceased to be a spiritual value." De-Christianizing tends to de-humanize. This becomes "a refined barbarism." Men are even used for anti-human ends, and dignity is obscured. Hence, "in making himself God, man has unmanned himself."[4] Berdyaev here attacks humanism and its cohorts.

Also, many modern novels fail to view man as a whole and disclose only parts of man especially for sensationalizing things, notably sex. Even the "heart" as the conscious center of feelings is neglected. Man becomes a function of sex rather than vice versa. Technology is also allowed to dehumanize man.[5] Much in creative philosophy is a much-needed reaction to this trend. For example, existential philosophy tries to recover the moral structure of being in concrete human existence. But some like Sartre and Heidegger miss the integral image of man, even as they fail to present a holistic picture. To them man's anxieties become more important than man himself. This promotes pessimism and despair, exaggerating despair negatively as Kierkegaard viewed it; for Søren Kierkegaard it was a more positive condition of penitence and faith. This common trend towards pessimism leads to nihilism, which Kierkegaard did not espouse.[6] Though he recognized the problem of despair he did not capitulate to it. Despair was to both Kierkegaard and Berdyaev akin to penitence, an influence on one's attitude and outlook.

The fault of a sociological democracy of a positivistic type is that it makes society supreme. Durkheim as a sociologist set the pace for this. Consequently, the masses fail to receive a qualitative leadership of a more aristocratic type. The view of progress is falsified, so Marx and Nietzche signify the end of humanism,[7] as cultural values are perverted under their economic theories. Capitalism is also a moral factor here, for it is losing influence while slipping more and more under state control; for instance, it cannot solve the problems of unemployment. Berdyaev is persuaded that a spiritual revolution is needed, so that personality's pre-eminent importance can be recovered along with moral values. A natural humanization of humanity is unattainable; it calls for a "spiritualization of society" through the Christian focus on God-manhood.[8]

Berdyaev could see that a rational knowledge of irrational elements of life is impossible; hence, such things as human will, intuition and the spirit of man must not be alienated from the problem of knowledge. Knowledge to Berdyaev was more than the relation of thought to being. It is an event in existence disclosing the mystery of being, even human being. This implies that being is not to be conceived as objective or exterior but as the interior condition of the knowing subject or self. Whenever the knowing subject objectifies a concept, as it may do under the influence of volition or emotion or illusion, it forms an object. This process of objectification becomes a state of disintegration, for it disrelates the knower from the existence and functions of the knower. Subjectivity and dignity are obscured.

Realism has overlooked this fallen state of man affecting the pseudo-projection of the object. It has failed to take into account the creativity of the knowing subject and its active contributions to both objectification and legitimate knowledge. The major error here is the failure to recognize the subject's falsifications through its objectifications upon projecting the object away from the subject. This erroneously externalizes all reality and stifles and stagnates existence as a creative product of subjectivity.[9]

It must be understood that subjectivity as referred to here is a spiritual mode of being that is essential to a person. Man is the meeting point of two worlds, the natural and the spiritual, the temporal and eternal. Berdyaev's anthropology is not limited to man as an object but is centered in man as a subject of the highest consciousness, one who transcends nature and even himself to an extent not only through self-consciousness but the existential questions surrounding it, such as: "Who am I," "What am I here for?" "What is the meaning of my life?" Kierkegaard posed such questions as basic to existential philosophy, and Berdyaev followed suit.

The "bourgeois mind" of the world gives man a peculiar consciousness of being. It is a view of being that is a "soullessness," says Berdyaev, which ravenously enjoys life as based on the ruins of past cultural achievements. Cultural progress is always followed by cultural deterioration. In Europe and America the old "spiritual culture of the West" based on sacred symbolism is being irrevocably annihilated mainly by machine-made businesses turned into false gods.[10]

Berdyaev sees this as a skepticism due to enslavement to visible material interests as opposed to the Absolute and eternal, which normally inspire working for the happiness of all men. Berdyaev states that the bourgeoisie works for a "hell on earth" while pretending to be preparing for "an earthly paradise" socialistically. Meanwhile the consciousness of sin and guilt is weakened as the things of eternity are ignored. A materialistic trend cannot defeat this bourgeois condition, for it is a spiritual matter of a distinctive type. There are no technical ends of life. The modern trend has been to allow our technical means to usurp the place of our cultural ends. This stifles the spirit and enslaves man to techniques, which do not represent our supreme values.

Berdyaev puts it forcefully like this: "We are confronted by a fundamental paradox: without techniques culture is impossible, its very growth is dependent upon it, yet a final victory of technique, the advent of a technical age brings the destruction of culture."[11] This is when great amounts of *things* are placed above values and man himself, whose very destiny in and beyond the world is thereby threatened. Thus a moral philosophy of technology is very much needed today. It must be correlated with Christian eschatology dignity, and the transfiguration of the world, says Berdyaev, and made basic to the action of the divine Spirit among men. Only by this can the cultural menace of the dominating machine be curtailed. The old culture threatened the body, the technological type threatens the heart. Technique makes everything a spiritual problem, for it needs the "spiritualization of life" through intensification of values. Only then can man preserve respect for the *imago dei* and his quality of life as Christian eschatology surmounts technological domination.[12]

As for its spread of contemporary civilization technology promotes another aspect of cultural enslavement. Berdyaev suggests that technological activity can be destructive of eternity," because of its power over life. The more comforts and conveniences we have the more complex our existence becomes. Yet the basic problem is man, who made the machine. He fails to link the machine to the highest spiritual ends and goals, yet new forms of creativeness can bring it about under spiritual inspiration and ethical responsibility.

Berdyaev senses how the doctrine of original sin has been used or misused to debase men socially. Often this is due to misguided critics, who fail to grasp the spiritual conceptions of Christianity. The perversion of Christianity leads to the debasement of man. But, as Berdyaev stresses, pure, unperverted Christianity preserves the dignity of man, it elevates rather than degrades man. Culturally, an important aspect of this is the fostering of human creativity. It promotes the seeking of the kingdom of heaven on earth, the perfect life of the fullness of love.[13] Christianity promotes the interaction of means and ends; therefore it decries the use of violence and hatred as means for attaining the perfect life. As cited by Berdyaev, the Russian thinker Vladimer Solovyev said, "It is impious to wait upon God to do that which simple justice could bring about."[14]

It was the Messianic nature of its faith that made Christianity capable of leading backward nations of the East to look toward a future goal and not stagnate, declares Berdyaev. Even the social utopias asserted in 19th century Europe were adaptations of the Christian doctrine of the Kingdom of God. In no way does Christian anthropology degrade man or his creative powers. Even those who rejected the Gospel profited much ethically from the regenerated conscience, which it stood for. "Christianity was the first to establish man's spiritual independence from Nature and the State . . ." The most important Christian teaching is that man is created *imago dei*. Man is more than a product of nature's processes, Berdyaev declares. "This higher nature of man as a free spirit could not have been destroyed and uprooted through original sin; the work of the Creator could not have been finally wiped out." Furthermore, it is by this that man is himself a type of creator who transcends nature. Belief in both God and man is implied; each moves toward the other in Christ. This is the basic peculiarity of Christianity as based upon God-manhood and the incarnation of the Spirit leading to the transfiguration of the world.[15]

The social failures and shortcomings of Christians today should not be imputed to their Gospel. Christianity, says Berdyaev, is the most difficult religion to practice. It is a "crucifixion of self." Though man received divine revelation he has found it hard not to impose upon it the limitations of his nature. Unlike other religions, however, Christianity does not flatter human nature but rather calls man to overcome his sinfulness through Christ-revealed Grace.[16] This opens up new surges of creativity, dignity and moral responsibility in most areas of life.

Marx tends to make of economic man an absolute. He also tends to deny personality. Both to him are functions of class and state. Man has no interior nature or dignity, for he is essentially an economic creature dependent upon class and the idea that personality is unreal. Marxism is strictly a materialistic philosophy. Human personality is merely a function of class while class is a function of economic production, which to Marx is the essence of reality. Marxism adapted Hegel's anti-personalist philosophy along with his dialectical method. By it the proletariat has come to regard itself not only as a class but as mankind itself.[17]

Berdyaev declares that "all classes are faulty," for their psychology opposes human brotherhood. The sense of sin is blunted by class interests and greed. The working men wish to join the bourgeoisie, and for this they cannot be blamed. Berdyaev says that all class mentality including the proletarian is bourgeois and desires to exploit things. Beneath this trend is a spiritual deterioration which looks solely to visible things as a denial of the invisible.[18] Underlying this is a materialistic philosophy or trend.

Christians must acknowledge the fact of class war and its perversion of values. Yet the Christian religion cannot establish a once-for-all economic system valid for all people everywhere for all time. It leaves social developments to human freedom. But the social relations between men are subject to the Church's criticism, especially the selfishness of competition and the economic materialization of depersonalized men. All forms of exploitation must be philosophically condemned and the laborers protected, for the value of personality is priceless to Christian principles. This applies critically not only to Communism but also to Capitalism. Both have ways of violating sacred values and depreciating personality. "The capital of financiers is collective and not personal," says Berdyaev adroitly. Christianity believes in the communality of personalities, he says, while abhorring impersonal social collectives of all sorts. The value and importance of labor are highly respected in relation to human creativity. It also subjects economic life in general to a spiritual principle with personality at the center of life expressing freedom of spirit and conscience, thought and creativity in work. Personality is superior in significance to either class, economic system or the state, because it belongs to an eternal world of spirit. Failure to respect this leads to the continued enslavement of man to sheer materialism.[19]

Yet philosophically capitalism is a moral problem. Basic is the fact that the laborer must sell his labor or means of production as a commodity. This deprives him of complete liberty, for he is under coercion, sometimes even of his re-conditioned conscience. In view of this, "class war," as it is called, should not be completely repudiated. It must be brought under spiritual principles. True Christianity cannot be determined by the class war. The latter must be resolved by the spirit. Neither socialism nor capitalism has priority in this respect. The bourgeois spirit is apt to succumb to either or both. Spiritual overcoming must be through the "renewal of souls," mainly among the workers. Needed is the "ennobling of society" by a "spiritual aristocracy," says Berdyaev, along with its democratization. A society of workers must have "an aristocratic principle." The latter implies a spiritual dignity or nobility, which is "the aristocracy of the sons of God."[20] This is not related to classism but to redemption under the Spirit. Berdyaev sees this akin to Feodorov's *Philosophy of Common Work* and ". . . the union of all human forces - scientific, economic, social, national and international - for one great task; the victory over nature and the defeat of death."[21]

Fundamental to such a society must be Sobornost or "togetherness" as basic to brotherhood. Christian philosophy must promote this on the side of the worker and promote the ennobling of the workingman even as it fosters the unity of all men.

Notes

1. Berdyaev, *The fate of Man In The Modern World*, S.C.M. Press, London, 1935, p. 15.

2. *Ibid*, section II, p. 16.

3. *Ibid*, pp. 21–25.

4. *Ibid*, p. 32. also see pp. 50, 80f, 90, 92.

5. Berdyaev, *Man And The Machine*.

6. *Ibid*, p. 38f.

7. *Ibid*, pp. 42f.

8. *Ibid*, p. 79f.

9. Berdyaev, *Spirit and Reality*, pp. 8–10, 31.

10. Berdyaev, *The Bourgeois Mind*, pp. 3, 10–13. N.Y., Sheed and Ward, Inc. 1934.

11. *Ibid*, pp. 14–32, 34.

12. *Ibid*, pp. 35–53.

13. *Ibid*, pp. 44–69.

14. *Ibid*, p. 70.

15. *Ibid*, pp.71–80.

16. *Ibid*, pp. 81–141.

17. Berdyaev, *Christianity and Class War*, N.Y. Sheed and Ward, 1933, pp. 11–18, 42ff.

18. *Ibid*, pp. 43, 48.

19. *Ibid*, pp. 50–83.

20. *Ibid*, pp. 57–108.

21. *Ibid*, pp. 109–111.

Chapter XIII

Subjectivity and Religion

Berdyaev's philosophy is basically a combination of the metaphysics of Spirit and his perspective of human existence. This combination amounts to a type of personalism and existentialism, a vigorous blend. Beyond Kierkegaard's emphasis upon personal anguish and dread as conditional to Christian redemption Berdyaev declared that man has an inner yearning for divine life, which implies the spirit of love.

Unlike Descartes' *cogito ergo sum* Berdyaev stresses *amo ergo sum*. In view of this, Berdyaev's personalist metaphysics is a yearning for and union with God, which is deemed by some to be more Christian than Kierkegaard's negative anguish or dread and what Heidegger secularizes as care or intentionality. Berdyaev makes this theme central to his work *Slavery and Freedom* while rejecting a "hierarchical personalism," as Edgar Munzer puts it with Max Scheler in mind.[1] In his great book, *The Destiny of Man*, Berdyaev sees the basic religious problem is man, not the cosmos or a theme like *sophia*. Sophiology, is intrinsic to his anthropology. Its emphasis is upon the supremacy of wisdom not only as human but as cosmically divine.

As a provocative ethicist Berdyaev amalgamates ideas from a variety of sources in order to blend with both Existenz philosophie and modern psychopathology. Personality is basic, so man is both the ethical and metaphysical problem, which demands an answer or solution. Ethics centers around the *theosis* of personality, not merely a theoretical set of the rules of conduct. Personal problems require existential solutions, not a universal legalism.

Psychiatry and psycho-pathology must not disregard the doctrine of original sin, says Munzer in behalf of Berdyaev. Man is inwardly divided, for his consciousness swings between the superconscious and the subconscious. Ethics, then, must be based upon more than the rules of conscious behavior.

Berdyaev thinks Dostoevsky was right in his work, *Man From The Underworld*, that basically man does not even aspire to happiness. This implies that hedonism does not provide us with a meaningful ethics. Munzer puts it this way: "Since ethics comprises man's superconscious destiny, anthropology culminates in eschatological ethics (related to) the doctrines of death, hell and paradise. If cosmic, historical, and existential times can be distinguished, hell is not eternity but only endless duration in non-existential time." In addition, "hell is non-being, non-creative and therefore a-eternal." True time is existential time when chronos or common historic time is qualitatively modified by eternity. Hell cannot be eternal. Traditional eschatology, which separates good and evil, ultimately denies the unity of creation. The Calvinist doctrine of pre-destination is absurd, says Berdyaev, who appeals positively to the cross and declares, "To conquer evil the good must crucify itself."[2] This is freely done, not deterministically.

Ethics is based upon personalist *theosis*, while history is communal theosis. In either case humanity looks ahead and is glorified in God. Berdyaev received support for this viewpoint from Solovyev's view of Sophia and included it in his book *The Meaning of History*. Since God and man meet in history and not only in the end, two kinds of history that are interrelated are celestial and terrestrial. They interpenetrate making for three types of processes, the cosmic, the human and the divine together with their related types of time: cosmic, historic and existential, respectively.

History becomes the mutual revelation of God and man to each other. By revelation historic time is transfigured into existential time while cosmic time is "no more," as suggested in Revelation 10:6. Existential time is "the eruption of eternity in time" comparable to the immeasurable or vertical invasion into the measurable or horizontal.[3] The spiritual precedent is God-in-Christ. Not a form of pantheism this is rather a pan-entheism.

In this respect for Berdyaev metaphysics and history coalesce, and personalistic anthropology is basic to their meeting. Freedom being of the nature of the metaphysical is the anthropological principle essential to comprehending history. Even the Fall is involved here, since it relates freedom to evil within history.

If *Moira* or fate were the destiny of man, there would be no goal for mankind; cosmic time would take over and obliterate freedom and the historic experiences related thereto. The same false notion of history underlies the monistic systems of German idealism and Marxism, which cater to Hellenic thought in or out of disguise.

Jewish thought was the first to deliver people from an objectified universal fate, which abandons man to natural forces. The Old Testament has an underlying motif that is the "metahistorical" goal of humanity. But Berdyaev declares that Jewish preoccupation with justice rather than immortality and eschatology led to the loss of theosis or a transfiguration of history and the union of man with God. A beatific state in this world was anticipated in theosis. The modern equivalent is a secular Marxist socialism based on an "aberrant Messianism" as Max Scheler and Christopher Dawson see it. It implies that society will come to "the reign of goodness on earth" whether religious or secular. But Berdyaev recognizes that "Christ's promise of beatitudes is from eternity, while realized in existential, not historic, time."[4] Thus *Kairos* anticipates the *eschaton*.

Munzer makes a significant appraisal when he says, "In his religious and metaphysical quest Berdyaev tries to overcome the spiritual impasse between Realism and Idealism by a creative union of *Sophia* and *Existenzphilosophie*. He is confronted with the problem of Philo, who wanted to unite Athens and Jerusalem, and of the great Scholastics who aspired to reconcile and delimit and spheres of Greek reason and Christian revelation. Like his predecessors, Berdyaev is not fully successful in this task." Perhaps Leo Chestov is right in regarding this problem as insoluble. For him Berdyaev's metaphysics, like few other philosopher's, is all the more reason to pay tribute to Berdyaev as one of the great "wrestlers with Christ."[5]

Berdyaev agreed with the Russian Orthodox perspective of the dissolution of naturalism related to "the impossibility of understanding man's moral life on the naturalistic basis."

Morality was viewed as a sphere of freedom apart from nature's causality. It was also evident that one could not have a reasonable basis for ethics beyond religion. A turning point in 19th century striving for ethical grounding was Tolstoy's *Confessions*. He stressed that man needs a personal and individual link with the divine absolute as a basis for his moral life. Also, Dostoevsky stressed that there is a hidden sub-conscious "underground" in the life of man, i.e. in the depths of the human soul there is "a dark, terrible abyss," from which we cannot extricate ourselves by morals alone. By this Dostoevsky shrewdly revealed the disorder in man, an inner sub-conscious chaos and helplessness reflecting "the need of a religious foundation for personal life."[6]

As intimated above, Berdyaev sees that the moral life of man as related to religion implies a freedom which supercedes total naturalism. Some thinkers abuse this view as though it implies a divine causation of man's choices, which makes God responsible for man's use of freedom. Berdyaev cannot condone this. He states it personally like this: "I have always protested against the idea that if God grants man moral freedom He is responsible for man's use of that freedom. Such an idea seems to me to contradict the very idea of freedom."[7] Berdyaev wanted both to protect freedom and to keep it responsible. When God created man He made him a co-creator "calling him to free spontaneous activity and not to formal obedience to His power." This free creativeness is both moral and of meonic freedom, which is not pre-determined or caused by God. Such creativeness is the creature's answer to the Creator's call, but in no way is it divinely coerced as in Calvinism. Man is not free if God perennially stands over him to compel obedience; he is free only if God's relation to him is that of giving him Grace. This implies that Grace seeks to increase freedom and to elevate it. Yet freedom alone cannot bring man to God and His Grace. Only Christ as the God-man can inspire the new life.[8] Christ is the Liberator.

Though religion at times has been a cause of dissension, true peace is above all an inner spiritual peace, which makes for unity. Religious exclusiveness is a disaster when a particular belief is posed as the universal or imposed exclusively. Culture is threatened apart from spiritual re-integration and ecumenicity. We need both "a spiritual supra-denominational-ism and supranationalism." The Gospel's law of love should not be limited to one's co-religionists. The Good Samaritan clearly expressed this. Berdyaev rightly criticizes race preju-dice and the practice of some Christians to detest non-Chris-tians. Some non-Christians may be closer to Christ than some Christians.[9]

Christian spirituality reaches beyond denominations; true Christianity promotes brotherhood only as it becomes more spiritual and ethically humanized. Christianity must defend man when the world does not. Too often religions have been called upon to bless the ruling classes. Sometimes atheistic movements have caused varieties of religious people to make for solidarity, who in more normal conditions would have wrangled with one another.[10]

Christians must proclaim that the world cannot be saved without Christ as Savior, but this does not mean that only those whose conscience is committed to him will be saved. Berdyaev puts it well, "Christ is also with those who are not with Him." He said, "I have sheep of other households." (folds).[11] "Chris-tians," said Berdyaev, "will have to speak more than ever be-fore of their own sins rather than of the sins of the world."[12] Whatever its forms, they need to work for the removal of "the poison of hate." Yet others have similar problems. Do they have better solutions? It's doubtful.

Though the New Testament speaks of three kinds of love, eros, philos and Agape, the latter alone spells a sacrificial, even suffering love that by divine inspiration gives to persons of faith the highest love, a self-giving love, which not only respects others but helps them in every respect to fulfill them-selves and overcome their temptations. Christian salvation is incomplete if it falls short of this quality of Christ-inspired love. Ethics is at its best when it is moved by this kind of love with its charitable motivations and outgoing expressions of sacrifice.

Notes

1. E. Munzer, *op cit*, pp. 191–193.

2. *Ibid*, pp. 193–195. Cf.

3. See Slaatte, *Time And Its End*, pp. 57, 58f.

4. Cf. E. Munzer, *op cit*, pp. 195–197.

5. *Ibid*, p. 198.

6. Visser t'Hooft, *A Traffic In Knowledge*, Student Christian Movement Press, London, 1934.

7. Berdyaev, *The Destiny of Man*, p. 32ff.

8. *Ibid*, pp. 32, 34, 36f.

9. Nicholas Berdyaev, "The Brotherhood of Man and The Religions," *World Fellowship of Faiths*, No. 4, bound pamphlets 1–24. The World Congress of Faiths (press), London, 1939. Cf. *Freedom And The Spirit* by Berdyaev, Chap. X

10. Berdyaev, *Spirit And Reality*, pp. 3–8, 10.

11. John 10:16.

12. Cited in *Time*, Vol. 51, April 5, 1948, p. 61.

Conclusion

Nicholas Berdyaev is one of the shrewdest ethicists of the twentieth century, and his philosophy helps prepare us for a creative plunge into the forthcoming blends of thought important to life in the twenty-first century.

Personhood is to Berdyaev the basic form of reality, for it is based upon the distinctiveness of human consciousness. Embraced by spirit it is the seat of mental, volitional, intuitive, emotional and religious types of thought while tributary to the holistic nature of human selfhood and its experiences in everyday existence. Personality becomes the center of concrete existence and, since it is more than individualistic, it is related to social and moral relationships essential to growth in personhood.

With imaginative zest personality frequently seeks and finds what is meant by creative thought and experience. Creativity becomes a powerful type of influence for good in all related activities including the arts and sciences as well as moral responsibilities and religious endeavors. Creativity proves to be the seat of constructive activity and inspiration to the individual who aspires to its fulfilled achievements. Wherever constructive works and leadership are called for, creativity is the bud and blossom of their achievements. Berdyaev saw creativity as the heart of human pursuits and regarded it as an essential aspect of personal growth and dignity as well as achievement.

Beneath the conscious selfhood of personality and its creativeness is the epistemological blend of sense perceptions and the first principles of reason essential to all knowledge. Basic to this is the phenomenological condition germane to knowledge and personal selfhood.

Ethically, consciousness is also fundamental to moral and spiritual insight and their applications to life from within concrete existence. Commonly overlooked by most people, even those of religious persuasion, is the place for meonic freedom as the underlying condition of all creation implying different possibilities for both God and man. The fall of man was an unusual possibility which to Berdyaev was not viewed as the corruption of human nature or the predisposition to sin and evil. As a condition it was more of a spiritual and social consequence than a predilection for sin or a sinful condition. In this respect Berdyaev sought to avoid any notions that made God responsible for evil, since he created man free to do either good or evil.

One of the main contributions to ethical understanding made by Berdyaev is his distinction between the major types of ethics: respectively, the moralistic, legalistic and redemptive types. Not only did he accentuate the place for the first two, while allowing also their misuse, philosophically, but primarily the redemptive type of ethics as based upon Christ-inspired Agape or self-giving love or sacrifice. Hence Berdyaev as a thinker became a strong Christian philosopher. Basic to this is what is religiously relevant existentially to the philosopher himself. Since he cannot evade the existential condition or the core of his existence as a conscious self he cannot avoid the positive influence of redemptive ethics upon his overall thought. In addition, Berdyaev saw how redemptive ethics is the answer to both personal problems and many contemporary social evils. The heart of this is the re-motivation of people by the love motif implicit in redemptive ethics. If Agape could be made more widespread the positive spirit and influence of redemptive ethics would become more well known and have a greater social impact throughout society. In promoting this socially the religious communities must accept a growing sense of responsibility, since secularism lacks the spirit for so doing.

Beneath these ethical concerns should be the awareness of subjectivity superceding objectivity. Not much really matters even in science if the knowing subject is violated, obscured or ignored. Without the concern for the knowing subject and its primacy the values basic to culture or a qualitative society could not develop or be retained. In addition, without concern for subjectivity in philosophy a thinker's thought is of negligible significance when it comes to promoting axiological ideas and maximum ethical effectiveness in society. Failure to give priority to the thinker is an anti-existential and anti-personalitic blunder. Similarly, religion is of little consequence if the personal roles of the believer and philosopher are ignored or violated. Without the subjective relevance of religious truths religion can be of little consequence, for the knowing subject is even essential to religious faith and its social impact. Objectively presented doctrines and principles are of little import without the subjective decisions of persons who find them of existential meaning and relevance to their lives.

Some interpreters perhaps wonder how and why Berdyaev arrived at the distinctiveness of redemptive ethics. The answer is that, despite the atheism of his Bolshevik background and its secular sentiments, he in time came to see that such a philosophy provided too weak an ethics. He eventually turned his back upon that kind of thinking, especially when he came to grasp the uniqueness of the revelation of Christ and the Christ-revealed love of God as a meaning-giving view of life with sacrificial Agape at its center. This philosophical awakening re-motivated Berdyaev quite like other people and provided him with a higher quality of life and ethical motivation both for personal life and intellectual pursuits. Berdyaev came to understand the Apostle's words: "God was in Christ reconciling the World" and, yes, "reconciling the world unto himself."

Bibliography

Berdyaev, Nicholas, "Marxism and the Conception of Personality," *Christendom*, Oxford (Blackwell) Vol. V, no. 20, December 1935. pp. 251–252.

————, *Ibid*, Vol. VI, no. 21, March 1936. pp. 35–40.

————, *Spirit and Reality*, New York: Charles Scribner's Son, 1939.

————, *The Bourgeois Mind*, New York: Sheed and Ward, Inc. 1934; De L'Esprit Bourgeois, Delachaux Et Niestle S.A., Paris VII, 1948.

————, *Christianity and Class War*, New York: Sheed and Ward, 1933.

————, "The Brotherhood of Man and the Religions," *World Fellowship of Faiths*, No. 4, bound pamphlets, 1–24, London: The World Company of Faiths press, 1939.

————, *Essai de Metaphysique Eschatologique*, Paris: Aubier Editions Montaigne, 1941.

————, *Towards A New Epoch*, London: Geoffrey Bles, 1949.

————, *The Divine and the Human*, London: Geoffrey Bles, 1949.

Berdiaff, N., "Communist Secularism," *Christianity and the Crisis*, London: Victor Gallancz Ltd., 1933.

————, "Le Philosophe et l'existence," *Actualites*, Scientifique at inductrielles, (533) IV.

————, "The Truth of Orthodoxy," *The Student World*, July 1928.

Berdyaev, Nicholas, *The End of Our Time*, New York: Sheed and Ward, 1933.

————, Article in *Time*, Vol. 51, April 5, 1948.

————, *The Beginning And The End*, London: Geoffrey Bles, 1949.

————, *Der Sinn des Schaffens*, Tubingen: 1927.

————, *Le Sens de l'acte createur*, Paris: *Esprit*, No. 8, August 1948.

————, *The Destiny of Man*, London: Geoffrey Bles, 1949.

Berdyaev, Nicholas, *Slavery and Freedom*, New York: Scribner Sons, 1944.

————, *Solitude and Society*, London: Geoffrey Bles Ltd., Centenary Press, 1947.

————, *Dream and Reality*, London: Geoffrey Bles, 1950.

————, *Freedom and the Spirit*, London: Geoffrey Bles, The Centenary Press, 1947.

————, *The Meaning of History*, New York: Scribner Sons, 1936.

————, "Christianity and Anti-Semitism," *Blackfriars*, Oxford: October 1948.

————, "War and the Christian Conscience," pamphlet, series *Pax Pamphlets*, No. 2. London: James Clarke and Co., Ltd. 1938.

————, "The Paradox of Falsehood," *Christendom*, Vol. IV, Oxford: Autumn 1939. No. 4.

————, "Marxism and the Conception of Personality," *Christendom*, Oxford: Vol. V, No. 21, March 1936.

————, Preface, Adolphe Lazareff, *Vie et Connaissance*.

————, *The Fate of Man In The Modern World*, London: SCM Press, 1935.

————, *Man and the Machine*.

Berdiaeff, N., "Christianity, Nationalism and the State," *World's Youth*, Vol. X, no. 3, Oct. 1934, Geneva, Switzerland: YMCA.

Buber, Martin, *I And Thou*, Edinburgh: T & T Clark, 1937.

Duddington, Natalie, "Philosophy In Russia, *"Philosophy*, Vol. VII, 1952.

Emmet, Dorothy M. "Kierkegaard and the Existential Philosophy," *Philosophy*, Vol. XVI, 1946, London: MacMillan & Co., Ltd.

Kierkegaard, Soren, *Journals of Kierkegaard*, ed. by Bretall, New York: Harper & Bros. 1951. Princeton University Press 1951.

Lampert, Evgueny, *Modern Christian Revolutionaris*, editor Donald Attwater.

Lewis, Edwin, *A Philosophy of the Christian Revelation*, New York: Harper and Bros. 1940.

Mounier, Emanuel, *A Personalist Manifesto*, London: Longman, Green and Co., 1938.

Pascal, Blaise, *Pensees and Provincial Letters*, New York: The Modern Library, 1941.

Porret, Eugene, "Un Grostique Moderne: Nicolas Berdiaeff," *For et Vie*, Paris: No. 2, 1938.

Slaatte, Howard A. *Time And Its End*, New York: Vantage Press, 1962. Landham, MD, University Press of America, 1980.

———, *Time, Existence and Destiny*, New York: Peter Lang, Inc. 1989.

———, *Modern Science and the Human Condition*. Santa Barbara, Calif., Intelman Books, 1974, also University Press of Am, 1981.

Visser t'Hooft, *A Traffic in Knowledge*, London: Student Christian Movement Press, 1934.

Victoroff, David, *Communism and Christians*, "The Christian Sources of Existentialism," Sobornost Series 3, no. 3, Summer, 1948.

Subject Index

agape 4, 10, 17, 20, 26, 54, 64f,
    89, 111, 114, 135, 140
anthropology 8, 11, 13, 40, 80, 82,
    95, 100, 120
awakening, spiritual 109, 125

Barthianism 29, 40, 60, 99
bourgeoisie 101, 117, 120, 124

capitalism 124f
classism 105, 124f
Communism 61, 70
conscience 5, 55, 63, 105
consciousness 7f, 9, 23, 49, 62,
    71, 77, 85, 91f, 110
creative acts 7, 15, 37f, 39, 63
creativeness 31f, 41, 122f, 137
creativity 36f, 39, 47, 58, 62

das Man 8, 19, 49
death 126f
dehumanization 117f, 124
depersonalization 110
despair 43, 50, 117
destiny 131f

economic issues 102
ecumenicity 88f
eschatology 121, 130
eternity 81, 85f
ethics, types 17, 21, 35, 69f
evil 117, 134
existentialism 33, 36, 39, 44, 47f,
    51f, 54, 59, 65, 70, 73f,
    75, 80f, 87, 109f, 120,
    129, 130, 132, 138f

faith 8, 16, 24, 77, 79, 87, 109,
    114
fall, the 9, 10f, 12, 17, 24, 28, 31f,
    48, 77, 79, 87, 109, 114
freedom 10, 11, 12, 15f, 24, 31,
    38, 50, 71, 73, 77, 82, 85,
    91, 94f, 97, 133, 191f

God-man 32, 70, 76f, 131, 146
Gnostisism 22f
Grace 10, 15f, 24, 82, 123, 134
greatness of man 7, 93

heart 36, 42, 53, 85, 100, 112, 118
Hegelianism 23, 25, 42, 99
Heidegger 10
history 131
Holy Spirit VII, 25, 27, 38, 41, 82,
    87, 101, 103, 110

"I AM" (Yahweh) 50f, 54
idealism 25, 32f, 53, 77f
imago dei 99, 103, 117, 121, 124

kairos, See eschatology and
    eternity.
Kant's ethics, See Kant in name
    index.

legalism 10, 52, 57f, 64, 86f, 92,
    103
Logos 27f, 32

Marxists VI, 89, 123f
meonic freedom 9, 42, 62, 72f,
    81, 85f, 93, 134, 138

Name Index

Adler, Alfred, 12f, 14
Augustine, 10, 43f, 67, 70, 76, 86, 94, 99f
Aquinas, 34
Arisstotle, 23, 45

Barry, Bishop F. R., 21f
Barth, Karl, 60, 99. See Barthianism in subject index.
Bloy, Leon, 84
Boehme, Jacob, 33, 35

Calvin, John, 86
Chestov, Leo, 109
Clement of Alexandria, 35

Descartes, Rene, 107ff
Dostoevsky, Fyodor, 10, 12, 74f, 108
Duddington, Natlie, 78
Duns Scotus, 26

Feodorov, 105
Fichte, Johann, 83
Freud, Sigmund, 99

Hartmann, Nicholas, 67
Hegel, C.F.W., 32f, 45, 68, 83, 94, 105
Heidegger, Martin, 10, 14, 43, 83, 99, 107

Ibsen, Henrik, 11, 14, 75, 83

Kant, Emmanuel, 5, 18, 28, 32, 53, 55, 57f, 68, 74, 104
Khomiakov, 76

Kierkegaard, Soren, 12, 14, 28, 33, 43f, 54, 67, 72, 101, 107, 109, 114, 116

Lampert, Evgueny, VIII, 86
Lewis, C.S., 13
Lewis, Edwin, 15, 65, 68f
Luther, Martin, 86

Marx, Karl, 12, 84, 100, 104, 148
Mascall, Eric, 60
Matheson, George, 43
Mourier, Emanuel, 41f, 51
Munzer, Edgar, 107f

Nietzsche, Friedrich, 32, 34, 54, 83, 101f, 104, 113

Pascal, Blaise, 8, 12, 46, 51, 67, 72, 95, 107
Plato, 46, 69
Plotimus, 61

Rapp, Madame, vii

Sartre, Jean-Paul, 45, 113
Scheler, Max, 107, 109
Schleiermacher, Friedrich, 27
Slaatte, Howard, A., 51, 70, 75
Socrates, 43, 75
Soloviev, Vladimer, 33, 35, 103, 108
Spinoza, Baruch, 85

Tolstoy, Leo, 12, 76, 86, 99, 101, 128
Tillich, Paul, 66, 69

Victoroff, David, 46, 50, 76

Wesley, John, 34f, 56, 59, 64